Marsh, Valerie.
Stories that stick :
quick and easy storyboar
c2002. WITHDRAWN
33305212056364
mh   03/02/07

Stories That Stick

Quick and Easy Storyboard Tales

Valerie Marsh

Illustrated by Patrick Luzadder

UpstartBooks

Fort Atkinson, Wisconsin

To our favorite stories and the memories
of the people who told them.

Published by **UpstartBooks**
W5527 Highway 106
P.O. Box 800
Fort Atkinson, Wisconsin 53538-0800
1-800-448-4887

© Valerie Marsh, 2002
Cover design: Debra Neu Sletten

The paper used in this publication meets the minimum requirements of American
National Standard for Information Science — Permanence of Paper for Printed Library
Material. ANSI/NISO Z39.48-1992.

All rights reserved. Printed in the United States of America.
The purchase of this book entitles the individual librarian or teacher to reproduce copies
for use in the library or classroom. The reproduction of any part for an entire school sys-
tem or for commercial use is strictly prohibited. No form of this work may be repro-
duced or transmitted or recorded without written permission from the publisher.

Contents

Introduction

Songs and Poems

Aesop's Fables

Folktales

Story Patterns   41

Introduction

Stories are powerful. Some stories are so memorable that they have stuck with you throughout your life. These are the stories in this book—the ones that you already know, the stories that stuck with you all this time. Telling these stories will be easy and fun, and, you can make the stories stick in children's memories by having the children help you stick the pictures on the storyboard as you share the story.

How to Use This Book

1. Choose a story that you want to tell. Each story begins with a list of all the pictures you need, and those pictures are keyed to a pattern in the back of the book.

2. Photocopy the story patterns from the back of the book. The benefit of having all the patterns together in one section is that you can literally cut the pages out of the book to more easily copy and work with them. The patterns are grouped by "Characters" and "Props and Scenery." Within these two groupings, you'll find all the people, animals and setting details you need to tell your story.

3. You may also use die-cut figures, ink stamps, tangram pieces (see page 88), or even oversized stickers on paper. Any common object (pertinent to your story) such as a cotton ball, ribbon, small dog bone, or paper cup can be mounted to your fasteners with glue.

4. Let the children help you color and cut out the pictures.

5. Laminate or cover pictures with clear contact paper (optional).

6. Create a folder for each story, and store the pictures and a copy of the story together for convenience and efficiency.

7. Attach fasteners. Depending on your storyboard, fasteners could be Velcro, magnetic tape, or flannel pieces. For larger pictures, place the fasteners in several different spots.

8. Review the story once or twice.

9. Tell the story, putting on or taking off pictures as you need them.

10. Retell the story. This time let the children help put the pictures up or take them down as the story unfolds. Give children a picture to hold until it is needed in the story.

Storytelling Rules

1. There are no rules.

2. Tell stories from this book that you like.

3. Keep it simple.

4. Relax and teach the story—don't perform it.

5. Encourage the children to get involved by putting up and taking down the pictures in the story.

6. Remember: children are listening for your story, not your mistakes.

7. Retell, retell, retell! Make the story picture sets available for children to retell to each other.

8. Enjoy!

Why Storytelling?

As children listen to a story, they use many skills to make sense of it and integrate it into their lives. Listening to and participating in the stories included in this book provides children opportunities for practicing a wide range of skills. These include:

- Using their imagination to create mental pictures of the tale;
- Developing their oral communication skills by hearing new words, phrases, and ideas;
- Refining auditory discrimination skills;
- Strengthening critical thinking skills;
- Growing their creative abilities;
- Expanding their active listening skills;
- Developing the fine motor skills of cutting and coloring;
- Strengthening sequencing skills;
- Distinguishing between reality and fantasy;
- Building self-confidence;
- Growing their love for books and reading.

These stories incorporate auditory, visual, and kinesthetic learning styles. The children are hearing you tell the story. They are seeing the pictures that go with the story. And they are putting up and taking down the pictures as the story unfolds.

Always be sure to repeat favorite stories. Sometimes in repeating a story, it will become a favorite, and each story deserves to be told at least twice. Of course, the best indicator of which stories to retell come from your audience. Children's requests for a particular story should be honored whenever possible.

The stories in this book can be used with a wide range of children. Some stories are very simple. After hearing the story once or twice, the students can tell it all by themselves. Other stories have a much higher degree of sophistication and can be used to introduce discussions of more complex issues. Several Aesop's fables are included here, which are known for communicating a moral or lesson, and discussion questions are provided at the end of each one. A 10-year-old listener brings different experiences and expectations to the story than does a six-year-old, and each listener and teller gains what they need to from the story at that particular moment. See what you and your listeners can discover!

Stories are powerful. When we see the rapt expression on a listening child's face or hear the unplanned sigh or laughter from listeners at a particularly sad or funny part of the story, we are witnessing the mysterious, magical, and timeless power of storytelling. Yes, they have such power that they stay with us long after we hear them. Stories stick.

Bear Hunt

Pictures Needed

- Pretty House (p. 82)
- Bridge (p. 80)
- Tall Grass (p. 73)
- River (p. 77)
- Mountain/Hill (p. 80)
- Cave (p. 79)
- Bear (p. 49)
- Boy (p. 41)

(Put the pretty house on the left side of the storyboard. Add pictures to the right side as you tell the story, and invite the children to do the following motions with you.)

(Make a walking sound by patting your legs with your hands.)

Going on a bear hunt.
Going on a bear hunt. **(Children repeat.)**

All right?
All right.

Let's go.
Let's go.

Coming to a bridge. **(Put bridge on board.)**
Coming to a bridge.

Can't go under it.
Can't go under it.

Can't go over it.
Can't go over it.

Can't go around it.
Can't go around it.

Gotta walk across it.
Gotta walk across it.

Okay?
Okay.

Alright?
Alright.

Let's go.
Let's go.

(Pound hands on chest to make thumping noise. Then continue patting legs with hands.)

Coming to some tall grass.
(Put tall grass on board next to bridge.)
Coming to some tall grass.

Can't go under it.
Can't go under it.

Can't go over it.
Can't go over it.

Can't go around it.
Can't go around it.

Gotta walk through it.
Gotta walk through it.

Okay?
Okay.

Alright?
Alright.

Let's go.
Let's go.

(Rub hands on legs to make swishing noises. Then, continue patting legs with hands.)

Coming to a river.
(Put river on the board next to tall grass.)
Coming to a river.

Can't go under it.
Can't go under it.

Can't go over it.
Can't go over it.

Can't go around it.
Can't go around it.

Gotta swim across it.
Gotta swim across it.

Okay?
Okay.

Alright?
Alright.

Let's go.
Let's go.
(Make swimming movements with arms. Then continue patting legs with hands.)

Coming to a mountain.**(Put mountain on board.)**
Coming to a mountain.

Can't go over it.
Can't go over it.

Can't go under it.
Can't go under it.

Can't go around it.
Can't go around it.

Gotta go through it.
Gotta go through it.

Okay?
Okay.

Alright?
Alright.

Let's go. **(Use a voice that sounds scared.)**
Let's go.

(Put cave on mountain. Close your eyes and put your hands in front of you. Act like you are feeling for something. Invite children to do these actions with you.)
I feel something cold and hard.
It must be the walls of the cave.
I feel something warm and furry.
It must be…
OH NO! IT'S A BEAR! **(Put bear in cave.)**
RUN!!!

(Pat legs at a faster rate.)
Coming to a mountain.
(Point to each picture as you come to it. Make climbing motions and noises.)

Coming to a river. Splash! Splash!
(Make swimming motions.)

Coming to some tall grass. Swish! Swish!
(Make swishing motions.)

Coming to a bridge! Thump! Thump!
(Make thumping motions.)

Keep running! The bear is right behind us!

Run!

Aahh…Here we are at home, safe from the bear.
(Put boy in house.)

The Bear Went Over the Mountain

Pictures Needed

- Mountain/Hill (p. 80)
- Bear (p. 49)
- Goat (p. 55)
- Pig (p. 59)
- Pictures from this book or die-cuts of a variety of objects

(As you sing "The Bear Went Over the Mountain" with the children, walk the bear up the mountain. When the bear gets to the top of the mountain, ask a child to place an object on the other side of the mountain. This is the object that the bear sees.)

(Put the bear and the mountain on the storyboard.)

The bear went over the mountain.
The bear went over the mountain.
The bear went over the mountain.
To see what he could see.

And all that he could see,
And all that he could see,
Was a **goat** on the side on the mountain.
A **goat** on the side of the mountain,
A **goat** on the side of the mountain,
Was all that he could see.

And all that he could see,
And all that he could see,
Was a **pig** on the side on the mountain.
A **pig** on the side of the mountain,
A **pig** on the side of the mountain,
Was all that he could see.

(Ask for children to choose another object to put on the other side of the mountain. Then, sing that verse. Continue as time permits.)

Eensy Weensy Spider

Pictures Needed

- Spider (p. 61)
- House with Waterspout (p. 82)
- Sun (p. 76)
- Rain Cloud (p. 76)

(Place house with waterspout, sun, and spider on storyboard.)

The Eensy Weensy Spider went up the waterspout.
(Move spider up the waterspout.)

Down came the rain,
(Put rain cloud on board. Remove sun.)

And washed the spider out.
(Move spider down the spout.)

Out came the sun and dried up all the rain.
(Put the sun up and remove the rain cloud.)

And the Eensy Weensy Spider climbed up the spout again.

Five Little Monkeys

Pictures Needed

- Five Monkeys (pgs. 57 and 58)
- Bed (p. 69)

(Place all monkeys and bed on storyboard. Invite children to do the hand motions with you as you recite the poem together.)

Five little monkeys jumping on the bed.
One fell off and broke his head.
Mother called the doctor and the doctor said,
"No more monkeys jumping on the bed."
(Make one monkey "jump" on bed and then fall off. Remove monkey from board.)

Four little monkeys jumping on the bed.
One fell off and broke his head.
Mother called the doctor and the doctor said,
"No more monkeys jumping on the bed."
(Make second monkey "jump" on bed and then fall off. Remove monkey from board.)

Three little monkeys jumping on the bed....

Two little monkeys jumping on the bed.....

One little monkey jumping on the bed.
One fell off and broke his head.
Mother called the doctor and the doctor said,
"That's what you get for jumping on the bed!!"

Variation: Begin reciting this poem rather loudly. With each verse, use a softer and softer voice. On "two little monkeys" use a whisper voice. When you get to the last verse, just mouth the words with the children. On the very last line, use a loud voice to say, "That's what you get for jumping on the bed!"

Hand Motions:

1. Five little monkeys jumping on the bed.
   ("Jump" five fingers of one hand up and down on palm of other hand.)

2. One fell off and broke his head.
   (Hold up one finger. Then, hold head in hands and shake back and forth.)

3. Mother called the doctor and the doctor said,
   (Pantomime making a phone call.)

4. No more monkeys jumping on the bed!
   (Shake finger as if scolding.)

Holiday Poems

Pictures Needed

- Fence (or Popsicle sticks) (p. 79)
- Pumpkins, or Jack-o'-Lanterns (p. 65)
- Turkeys (p. 62)
- Reindeer (p. 59)
- Snowmen (p. 48)
- Leprechauns (p. 46)
- Bunnies (p. 50)

Five Fat Pumpkins

(Before beginning poem, place fence on the storyboard. Then put all five pumpkins, or turkeys, etc., on the fence. Remove pumpkins as you recite the poem.)

Five fat pumpkins sitting on a gate,

The first one said, "Oh my, it's getting late.

The second one said, "There are owls in the air."

The third one said, "We don't care."

The fourth one said, "Let's run and run and run."

The fifth one said, "Until Halloween is done."

Whhooooo went the wind,

And out went the light,

And those five fat pumpkins rolled out of sight.

Five Fat Turkeys

Five fat turkeys sitting on a gate,

The first one said, "Oh my, it's getting late."

The second one said, "There are cooks everywhere."

The third one said, "We don't care."

The fourth one said, "Let's run and run and run."

The fifth one said, "Until Thanksgiving day is done."

Whhooooo went the wind,

And out went the light,

And those five fat turkeys gobbled out of sight.

Gobble, Gobble, Gobble.

Five Fat Reindeer

Five fat reindeer sitting on a gate,

The first one said, "Oh my, it's getting late."

The second one said, "There are presents everywhere."

The third one said, "We don't care."

The fourth one said, "Let's fly and fly and fly."

The fifth one said, "Until holidays are done."

Whhooooo went the wind,

And out went the light,

And those five fat reindeer flew out of sight.

Five Fat Snowmen

Five fat snowmen sitting on a gate,

The first one said, "Oh my, it's getting late."

The second one said, "There is sunshine every-where."

The third one said, "We don't care."

The fourth one said, "Let's run and run and run."

The fifth one said, "Until warm weather is done."

Whhooooo went the wind,

And out went the light,

And those five fat snowmen melted out of sight.

Five Fat Leprechauns

Five fat leprechauns sitting on a gate,

The first one said, "Oh my, it's getting late."

The second one said, "There are shamrocks everywhere."

The third one said, "We don't care."

The fourth one said, "Let's run and run and run."

The fifth one said, "Until St. Patty's Day is done."

Whhooooo went the wind,

And out went the light,

And those five fat leprechauns scampered out of sight.

Five Fat Bunnies

Five fat bunnies sitting on a gate,

The first one said, "Oh my, it's getting late."

The second one said, "There are Easter eggs everywhere."

The third one said, "We don't care."

The fourth one said, "Let's hop and hop and hop."

The fifth one said, "Until Easter day is done."

Whhooooo went the wind,

And out went the light,

And those five fat bunnies hopped out of sight.

In a Dark, Dark House

Pictures Needed

- House needed for all versions. Individual items for specific months listed with stories. You may use the dark house pattern on p. 83 or a die-cut or house cut from wallpaper.

(In all versions, add pieces listed as they are mentioned.)

In a Dark, Dark, September House

- Plate (p. 68 or die-cut circle)
- Apple (p. 64 or die cut)

In a dark, dark woods,
there was a dark, dark path.

And down that dark, dark path,
there was a dark, dark house.

And in that dark, dark house,
there was a dark, dark hallway.

And down that dark, dark hallway,
there was a dark, dark pantry.

And in that dark, dark pantry,
there was a dark, dark plate.

And in that dark, dark plate,
There was a crisp, crisp…apple!

In a Dark, Dark, October House

- Closet Door (p. 70)
- Bag (p. 66 or piece of brown paper sack)
- Candy (p. 66 or candy piece)

In a dark, dark woods,
there was a dark, dark path.

And down that dark, dark path,
there was a dark, dark house.

And in that dark, dark house,
there was a dark, dark hallway.

And down that dark, dark hallway,
there was a dark, dark room.

And in that dark, dark room,
there was a dark, dark closet.

And in that dark, dark closet,
there was a dark, dark bag.

And in that dark, dark bag,
There was a sweet, sweet…piece of Halloween candy!

In a Dark, Dark, November House

- Oven (p. 67)
- Roasted Turkey (p. 67 or die cut)

In a dark, dark woods,
there was a dark, dark path.

And down that dark, dark path,
there was a dark, dark house.

And in that dark, dark house,
there was a dark, dark hallway.

And down that dark, dark hallway,
there was a dark, dark kitchen.

And in that dark, dark kitchen,
there was a dark, dark oven.

And in that dark, dark oven,
There was a juicy, juicy…Turkey!

In a Dark, Dark, December House

- Christmas Tree (p. 74 or die cut)
- Present (p. 70 or die cut)

In a dark, dark woods,
there was a dark, dark path.

And down that dark, dark path,
there was a dark, dark house.

And in that dark, dark house,
there was a dark, dark hallway.

And down that dark, dark hallway,
there was a dark, dark living room.

And in that dark, dark living room,
there was a bright, bright tree.

And underneath that bright, bright tree,
There was a big, big…Present!

In a Dark, Dark, January House

- Refrigerator (p. 67)
- Snowman (p. 48)

In a dark, dark woods,
there was a dark, dark path.

And down that dark, dark path,
there was a dark, dark house.

And in that dark, dark house,
there was a dark, dark hallway.

And down that dark, dark hallway,
there was a dark, dark kitchen.

And in that dark, dark kitchen,
there was a dark, dark refrigerator.

And in that dark, dark refrigerator,
There was a white, white…Snowman!

In a Dark, Dark, February House

- Closet Door (p. 70)
- Valentine (p. 71 or die cut or valentine card)

In a dark, dark woods,
there was a dark, dark path.

And down that dark, dark path,
there was a dark, dark house.

And in that dark, dark house,
there was a dark, dark hallway.

And down that dark, dark hallway,
there was a dark, dark living room.

And in that dark, dark living room,
there was a dark, dark closet.

And in that dark, dark closet,
There was a red, red…Valentine!

In a Dark, Dark, March House

- Closet Door (p. 70)
- Leprechaun (p. 46 or die cut)

In a dark, dark woods,
there was a dark, dark path.

And down that dark, dark path,
there was a dark, dark house.

And in that dark, dark house,
there was a dark, dark hallway.

And down that dark, dark hallway,
there was a dark, dark living room.

And in that dark, dark living room,
there was a dark, dark closet.

And in that dark, dark closet,
There was a green, green…Leprechaun!

In a Dark, Dark, April House

- Closet Door (p. 70)
- Basket (p. 68)
- Bunny (p. 50)

In a dark, dark woods,
there was a dark, dark path.

And down that dark, dark path,
there was a dark, dark house.

And in that dark, dark house,
there was a dark, dark hallway.

And down that dark, dark hallway,
there was a dark, dark bedroom.

And in that dark, dark bedroom,
there was a dark, dark closet.

And in that dark, dark closet,
there was a deep, deep basket.

And in that deep, deep basket,
There was a fuzzy, fuzzy…Bunny!

I Went Walking

Pictures Needed

- Walking Boy or Walking Girl (p. 42)
- Cow (p. 51)
- Pig (p. 59)
- Goat (p. 55)
- Chicken (p. 51)
- Dog (p. 52)
- Cat (p. 50)
- Other animal pictures

(Put picture of walking child on the storyboard.)

The storyteller says, "I went walking and what did I see?" **(Move the child along the board. Ask children to choose pictures to put on the board next.)**

Child answers, "I saw a big cow walking behind me," **(Child puts his/her picture behind the picture of the boy.)**

The storyteller says, "As I went walking, I saw a cow walking behind me. So I kept walking and what else did I see?"

Choose a second child who answers, "I saw a big cow walking behind me. Then I saw a fat pig walking behind me." **(Child puts picture of pig on board behind cow.)**

The storyteller says, "As I went walking, I saw a cow walking behind me. Then I saw I pig walking behind me. So I kept walking and what else did I see?"

(Based on interest and time available, continue asking children to add to the parade of animals.)

Old McDonald Had a Farm

Pictures Needed

- Farmer/Father (p. 45)
- Barn (p. 81)
- Cow (p. 51)
- Pig (p. 59)
- Goat (p. 55)
- Chicken (p. 51)
- Sheep (p. 60)
- Cat (p. 50)
- Dog (p. 52)

(Put the farmer and the barn on the storyboard. As you begin singing the song, add the farm animal that you are singing about.)

Old McDonald had a farm — E-I-E-I-O
And on his farm, he had a cow — E-I-E-I-O
With a "moo-moo" here and a "moo-moo" there,
Here a "moo" there a "moo"
Everywhere a "moo-moo"
Old McDonald had a farm — E-I-E-I-O
(Put a cow on the board.)

Old McDonald had a farm — E-I-E-I-O
And on his farm, he had a pig — E-I-E-I-O
With an "oink-oink" here and an "oink-oink" there,
Here an "oink" there an "oink"
Everywhere an "oink-oink"
Old McDonald had a farm — E-I-E-I-O
(Put a pig on the board.)

(Ask the children to add other animals to your song.)

Marching

Pictures Needed

Seasonal listed below or die-cuts

- Ghosts (p. 47)
- Turkeys (p. 62)
- Reindeer (p. 59)
- Santas (p. 48)
- Snowmen (p. 48)
- Valentines (p. 71)
- Leprechauns (p. 46)
- Bunnies (p. 50)

Children will love doing this poem with every holiday. Get them to think of other objects that could be substituted in. You can have lots of fun talking with different voices.

Ghosts

(Use a floating voice. Place correct amount of ghosts on board when indicated. Pumpkins can be substituted for ghosts if desired.)

The ghosts they are floating,

They're floating down the hall,

They're floating on the ceiling,

They're floating on the wall,

They're floating two by two,

They're floating four by four,

You say you cannot see them?

Look out! Here come some more!

Turkeys

(Use a gobbling voice.)

The turkeys they are gobbling,

They're gobbling down the hall,

They're gobbling on the ceiling,

They're gobbling on the wall,

They're gobbling two by two,

They're gobbling four by four,

You say you cannot see them?

Look out! Here come some more!

Reindeer

(Make up a reindeer voice.)

The reindeer they are flying,

They're flying down the hall,

They're flying on the ceiling,

They're flying on the wall,

They're flying two by two,

They're flying four by four,

You say you cannot see them?

Look out! Here come some more!

Santas

(Use a deep, Ho, Ho, Ho voice.)

The Santas they are laughing,

They're laughing down the hall,

They're laughing on the ceiling,

They're laughing on the wall,

They're laughing two by two,

They're laughing four by four,

You say you cannot see them?

Look out! Here come some more!

Snowmen

(Make up a snowman voice.)

The snowmen they are melting,

They're melting down the hall,

They're melting on the ceiling,

They're melting on the wall,

They're melting two by two,

They're melting four by four,

You say you cannot see them?

Look out! Here come some more!

Valentines

(Use a love-filled voice.)

The valentines they are marching,

They're marching down the hall,

They're marching on the ceiling,

They're marching on the wall,

They're marching two by two,

They're marching four by four,

You say you cannot see them?

Look out! Here come some more!

Leprechauns

(Use squeaky voice.)

The leprechauns they are marching,

They're marching down the hall,

They're marching on the ceiling,

They're marching on the wall,

They're marching two by two,

They're marching four by four,

You say you cannot see them?

Look Out! Here come some more!

Bunnies

(Make up a rabbit voice.)

The bunnies they are hopping,

They're hopping down the hall,

They're hopping on the ceiling,

They're hopping on the wall,

They're hopping two by two,

They're hopping four by four,

You say you cannot see them?

Look Out! Here come some more!

Belling the Cat

Pictures Needed

- Large House (p. 85–87, or outline of house cut from wallpaper)
- Mice (p. 56) (one for each child if possible)
- Cat (p. 50)

Once there was a house. **(Put the large house on the storyboard.)**

There were lots of mice that lived in this house. **(Invite a child to help you put up the mice in the house.)**

There was also a cat that lived in this house. **(Put the cat in the house.)**

This cat had very sharp claws and very long whiskers. Every cat has sharp claws and long whiskers, doesn't it? But this cat was different. Do you know what made this cat different? It was his feet. This cat **(Point to the cat again.)** had super-soft feet. He could walk soooo silently.

This cat had one thing that he loved to do more than anything else in the world. Do you know what that was? **(Ask children for their ideas.)**

Yes, this cat loved to chase and catch mice!

Every mouse in this house was terrified that they would be the next mouse to be caught. **(Point to house and mice again.)** One evening, the mice had a meeting to figure out a way to keep from being caught by the cat. **(Move cat outside of house.)**

One mouse said, "The cat has such big feet that he can sneak up on any one of us so quietly and quickly. What can we do so that we can know when the cat is near?" **(Move the mice around as they are talking to each other.)**

Another mouse said, "Yes, we need a warning that the cat is coming."

The first mouse said, "I know! Let's put a bell around the cat's neck. Then we will be able to hear her coming and we can run and hide."

"Great idea!" said the mice.

"But who wants to put the bell around the cat's neck?" asked one mouse.

At the same time the other mice said, "Not I, not I, not I!"

To this day, that sneaky cat still does not have a bell around her neck.

☼ Discussion Questions ☼

- How many of you have cats at home? Does your cat have a bell on its collar? Why is that?

- How many of you have taken the risk to make something better? What was the result?

The Boy Who Cried Wolf

Pictures Needed

- Shepherd Boy (p. 41 or photograph)
- Mountain (p. 80)
- Sheep (p. 60 or cotton balls)
- Wolf (p. 63 or piece of fake fur)
- Woodcutter (p. 43)
- Fisherman (p. 43)

This is the shepherd boy. **(Place shepherd boy on storyboard.)**

One day he said, "Boring, boring, boring, that's what this job is. Everyone else has fun in his job but me. I am tired of climbing this same mountain every morning." **(Place mountain on board.)**

"I am tired of watching sheep all day. Nothing ever happens. Every morning the sheep go up the mountain to eat grass. All day long the sheep eat the grass. Every evening the sheep go down the mountain." **(Place the sheep on board.)**

"Every day, it's the same old thing, same old thing. Up the mountain, eat the grass, down the mountain. Up the mountain, eat the grass, down the mountain. Over and over again. I am going crazy! I wish something would happen!" **(Move sheep up the mountain. Pause them at the top. Then move the sheep down the mountain.)**

The next morning the shepherd boy had an idea. His idea would make his life more exciting. So as soon as the sheep got up to the top of the mountain, the shepherd boy started yelling, "Wolf! Wolf! Wolf! Wolf! A wolf is eating my sheep!" **(Move the shepherd boy and the sheep to the top of the mountain.)**

A woodcutter came running out of the woods and up the mountain. A fisherman came running from the lake and up the mountain. "We will help you. Where is the wolf?" **(Climb the woodcutter and fisherman up the mountain.)**

The boy laughed, "Ha, ha, ha. I tricked you. There is no wolf. I just wanted to see if you would come."

The fisherman and the woodcutter were not happy. "Do not trick us again." **(Move the woodcutter and the fisherman down the mountain.)**

But the next day, the shepherd boy was bored and so he decided to play the same trick again. Again he yelled, "Wolf! Wolf! Wolf! Wolf! A wolf is eating my sheep."

The woodcutter came running out of the woods and up the mountain. The fisherman came running from the lake and up the mountain. "We will help you. Where is the wolf?" **(Climb the woodcutter and fisherman up the mountain.)**

The boy laughed, "Ha, ha, ha. I tricked you again. There is no wolf. I just wanted to see if you would come again."

The fisherman and the woodcutter were very angry. "Do not trick us any more." **(Move the woodcutter and the fisherman down the mountain.)**

The next day the shepherd boy was bored again so he decided to play the same trick again. But just as he opening his mouth to yell "Wolf," there really was a wolf! It was a real wolf, with sharp, shiny teeth and long, pointy claws. And he looked very, very hungry. **(Put wolf on board.)**

The shepherd boy ran down the mountain and yelled, "Wolf! Wolf! Wolf! Wolf! A wolf is eating my sheep! A real wolf! Really! Really! Really! This is not a trick!" **(Put the shepherd boy next to he woodcutter and fisherman. Slide a sheep under the wolf as if he is eating it.)**

The woodcutter and fisherman heard the shepherd boy yelling. But they did not come running They did not help. They thought it was just another trick. They said, "Wolf? You are tricking us again. We will not help you. There is no wolf."

The shepherd boy begged, "Please, please help me. There really is a wolf this time. I am not tricking you."

But they did not believe him. So the shepherd boy climbed back up the mountain. The wolf was gone, and so was one of his sheep.

The shepherd thought about the tricks that he had played and made a decision. He decided that he would never again falsely cry wolf.

Discussion Question

- What do you think the shepherd boy learned?

The Dog and His Shadow

Pictures Needed

- Dog (p. 52)
- Dog Bone (p. 64 or real dog treat)
- Bridge (p. 80)
- Water (p. 77 or aluminum foil)

Far ago there was a dog. **(Put dog on storyboard.)**

This dog had a bone. **(Put the dog bone in the dog's mouth.)** It was a small bone but it smelled tasty. All day the dog had looked forward to sitting down and having a nice long chew on his bone.

But he had to cross the bridge to get home. **(Put the bridge on the board.)**

As the dog walked across the bridge, he happened to glance down into the water. **(Place the water under the bridge.)**

When the dog looked down into the water, he saw another dog! This dog had a bone in its mouth. The dog on the bridge looked very carefully at the dog in the water. The dog muttered to himself, "That dog in the water has a bigger bone than I do. And his bone looks juicier. I want his bone! I'll just jump in the water and take his bone."

The dog dropped his bone. **(Put dog bone in water under bridge.)**

The dog jumped into the water. But as soon as he did, the other dog and his bone disappeared!

☼ Discussion Questions ☼

- Who was the other dog in the water?
- Did the other dog really have a bigger bone?
- Should the dog have been satisfied with the bone he already had?

The Fox and the Grapes

Pictures Needed

- Fence (p. 79 or Popsicle sticks)
- Grapes (p. 64 or circles of foam)
- Fox (p. 53 or fake fur shape)

Far ago there was a fence. **(Put fence on storyboard.)**

A beautiful, tasty-looking bunch of grapes hung on this fence. **(Put grapes at the top of the fence.)**

Just then a hungry fox walked by. **(Put the fox near the grapes.)**

He spied those grapes glistening in the sun. Yum, yum, yum! Those grapes looked soooo tasty and the fox was soooo hungry.

The fox jumped up to grab the grapes. **(Move fox up and down as if he is jumping.)**

But the fox could not reach the grapes. They were just out of his bite. He jumped forward. He jumped sideways. He jumped backwards. He jumped again and again. He hopped. He swung his tail at those grapes. He blew as hard as he could on them. But the fox just could not knock them down.

Finally, the fox walked away in frustration. He muttered to himself, "Those grapes looked tasty. But I'll bet they're actually sour. I did not want them anyway."

☺ Discussion Questions ☺

- Why did the fox change his opinion of the grapes?
- Do you think the grapes really were sour?
- Have you ever heard the term "sour grapes"?

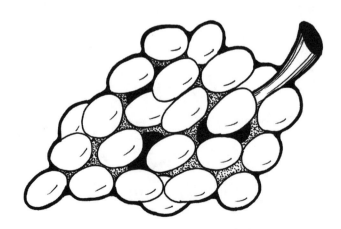

The Fox and the Stork

Pictures Needed

- Large House (p. 85–87)
- Fox (p. 53 or piece of fake fur cloth)
- Stork (p. 61 or large feather)
- Plates (p. 68 or small paper plates)
- Tall Glasses (p. 68 or small paper cups)

Once a tricky fox invited a stork over to his house for dinner. **(Put large house on storyboard. Put fox in it.)**

Fox put all of the food on two flat plates. When Stork arrived at Fox's house, he invited her to sit down at the table. **(Put stork on board.)**

Then he brought out the two plates filled with tasty food. **(Put plates on board.)** Fox started to eat, but Stork did not.

"Eat, friend Stork, eat! Why aren't you eating any of this tasty food that I have prepared for you?" asked Fox.

Stork replied, "Fox, your food looks very delicious, but you know that I cannot eat from that flat plate. My beak does not work like that."

Fox laughed, "Ha, ha, ha. What a funny trick I played on you, Stork. If you are not going to eat the tasty food that I prepared for you, then I will."

Fox ate all of Stork's food and Stork went home hungry that evening. **(Take all pictures off board.)**

But then it was Stork's turn to invite Fox to dinner. **(Put house back on board. Put stork in house.)**

When Fox arrived at Stork's house, he was very hungry and the delicious smells coming from Stork's kitchen made him even more hungry. **(Put fox in house.)**

Stork said, "Please sit down friend Fox, and I will bring out the food."

Fox sat down. He could hardly wait. Stork came out with two very tall glasses filled with food. She put one in front of Fox. The glass was so tall that Fox could not even see over the top of it. **(Put tall glasses on board.)**

Stork started eating and pretended not to notice that Fox was having a problem. Finally she said, "Eat, friend Fox, eat. Why aren't you eating any of this tasty food that I have prepared for you? Well, if you don't mind, this food is so delicious, that I will eat yours too."

It was then that Fox realized that he had been paid back with his own trick! And, it was now Fox's turn to go home hungry.

☼ Discussion Questions ☼

- Should Fox have been surprised by Stork's return trick?
- Was this a funny trick, or a not-so-nice trick?

The Lion and the Mouse

Pictures Needed

- Mouse (p. 56 or animal cracker)
- Lion (p. 55 or fake fur shape with two sticker dots of eyes)
- Net (p. 78 or plastic mesh fruit bag)

A tiny mouse was running home one day and not really looking where he was going. **(Put the mouse on the board.)**

He tripped over a big lion's paw. **(Put the lion on the board.)**

Lion roared and smacked his paw down on Mouse's tail. "How dare you wake me up from my nap?"

"Please don't eat me. Please let me go. If you let me go, I promise that someday I will help you," said the mouse.

"I will let you go Mouse, because you are too small to eat. But you are also too small to ever help me," said Lion.

As Mouse scampered away, he called back to Lion, "I will help you someday, Lion. I just know I will."

A few days later, all the animals in the jungle heard a terrible roaring. They all came running, including Mouse. There was Lion, caught tightly in a strong net. **(Put net over lion.)**

Little Mouse popped up. "I can help you, Lion. I told you that I would help you someday. Here is my chance."

Lion roared, "How can you help me? Can't you see that I am stuck in this strong net?"

"Yes, I can see that. Just hold still and I will get you out." Mouse started to chew on the strong ropes. His tiny, sharp teeth cut through the ropes in the net. After several minutes, Mouse had made a hole big enough for Lion to squeeze through. **(Move net away from lion.)**

"Thank you, Mouse. You and your sharp teeth saved my life," said the surprised lion.

Mouse replied, "Oh, you are welcome, Lion. I am glad that I could help you."

☼ Discussion Questions ☼

- What would have happened to Lion if he had eaten Mouse earlier?

- Do you think the other animals in the jungle were as surprised as Lion?

The Tortoise and the Hare

Pictures Needed

- Hare (p. 63)
- Tree (p. 74)
- Tortoise (p. 50)
- Clothesline (p. 75)

Hare had nothing to do. It was hot outside and he was so bored just napping under his favorite shade tree. **(Put hare and tree on the board, with the hare under the tree.)**

Just then Tortoise crawled by. He was creeping along so slowly that he was hardly moving at all. **(Put tortoise on board and walk him by hare.)**

Hare opened one eye when he heard Tortoise. He said, "Hey there, Tortoise. Could you go any slower? Or are you at top tortoise speed? I bet you started your trip 10 years ago."

Tortoise just kept on shuffling along, slowly, slowly. He looked at Hare and said, "Hare, I just keep moving on. I am going to get there when I get there. So, do you want to race?"

Hare laughed, "Me? Race you? You've got to be kidding! Wherever you are going, I will definitely get there faster than you. Sure, I will race you."

Tortoise said, "Just race me down to that clothesline."

Hare replied, "Tortoise, just to be nice, I will give you a head start. I was going to take a nap anyway. So, you just go ahead and start the race and I will catch up to you after my nap. In fact, I will pass you and win our race." **(Put clothesline on board between two trees.)**

Tortoise kept on walking and Hare went to sleep. Hare slept a long time. All that time

Tortoise shuffled along at his slow pace. At last, Hare woke up and stretched. As he finished stretching, he suddenly remembered that he was supposed to be racing Tortoise to the clothesline.

Hare dashed off toward the clothesline as fast as he could. But Hare was too late. Just as Hare got there, Tortoise walked under the clothesline. Tortoise had won the race! **(Move tortoise past the clothesline, and place hare behind him.)**

Tortoise said, "Hare, I knew I could win this race. And I did!"

Discussion Questions

- Do you think that the Hare was overconfident and careless?

- Do you think that Hare should have raced first, then taken his nap?

Three Billy Goats Gruff

17

Pictures Needed

- Bridge (p. 80)
- Hill/Mountain (p. 80)
- Troll (p. 46)
- Small Goat (p. 55)
- Middle Goat (p. 54)
- Large Goat (p. 54)

Far ago there was a bridge. **(Put the bridge and the hill on the storyboard.)** And there was a hill.

And there was a mean, hungry troll who lived under the bridge. **(Put the troll under the bridge.)**

One day, the small billy goat went trip, trapping across the bridge. He wanted to go across the bridge and up the hill to eat the fresh, green grass. His tiny footsteps sounded across the bridge. Trip, trap, trip, trap. **(Put the small goat on the bridge. Use a small voice for the footsteps.)**

Suddenly the mean old troll jumped out from under the bridge. **(Put the troll on the bridge.)**

"Who is that walking across my bridge?" growled the troll.

"It is only me, the smallest billy goat," answered the goat in a teeny, tiny voice.

"You are very small, little billy goat. But you look tasty. I am going to eat you up!" snarled the mean, old troll.

"Oh, don't eat me. Wait for my middle billy goat brother to come along. Then you can eat him.

He is bigger and tastier than I am," said the little billy goat.

The troll answered, "Oh, alright. Go on up the hill and eat the grass. I will wait for your bigger brother." **(Put the hill on the other side of the bridge. Move the little goat to the hill.)**

The next day, the middle billy goat went trip, trapping across the bridge. He wanted to go across the bridge and up the hill to eat the fresh, green grass. His middle-sized footsteps sounded quite loud as he walked across the bridge. Trip, trap, trip, trap. **(Put the middle goat on the bridge. Use a medium-sized voice for the footsteps.)**

Suddenly the mean old troll jumped out from under the bridge. **(Put the troll on the bridge.)**

"Who is that walking across my bridge?" yelled the troll.

"It is me, the middle billy goat," answered the goat in a stern, confident voice.

"You are bigger than your brother, middle billy goat. And you look tastier. I am going to eat you up!" growled the mean, old troll.

"Oh, don't eat me. Wait for my biggest billy goat

brother to come along. Then you can eat him. He is much bigger and tastier than I am," said the middle billy goat.

The troll answered, "Oh, alright. Go on up the hill and eat the grass with your little brother." **(Put the middle goat next to the little goat on the hill.)**

Later that evening, the largest billy goat went trip, trapping across the bridge. He wanted to go across the bridge and up the hill to eat the fresh, green grass. His huge footsteps sounded like thunder as he walked across the bridge. Trip, trap, trip, trap. **(Put the large goat on the bridge. Use a large voice for the footsteps.)**

Suddenly the mean old troll jumped out from under the bridge. **(Put the troll on the bridge.)**

"Who is that walking across my bridge?" growled the troll.

"It is me, the largest billy goat," answered the goat in a deep, gravelly voice.

"You are very large, indeed, billy goat. And you look tasty. I am so hungry! So, I am going to eat you up right now!" yelled the mean, old troll.

"Oh, you can't eat me. I am too big for you," said the largest billy goat. "But you can try. Come here and try."

The troll took a step towards the billy goat. **(Move the troll to the billy goat.)**

But the billy goat turned and kicked the troll back into the river. **(Make the troll fall into the water.)**

Then, the largest billy goat walked across the bridge and up the hill to eat the grass with his brothers. **(Finish walking the large goat across the bridge and up the hill.)**

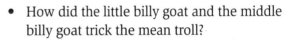

☺ Discussion Questions ☺

- How did the little billy goat and the middle billy goat trick the mean troll?

- Was the troll very smart?

Gingerbread Man

Pictures Needed

- Large House (p. 85–87)
- Boy (p. 41)
- Wife/Mother (p. 45)
- Farmer/Father (p. 45)
- Oven (p. 67)
- Gingerbread Man (p. 47)
- Cow (p. 51)
- Pig (p. 59)
- Chicken (p. 51)
- Fox (p. 53)

(Put the large house on the storyboard.)

Far ago, there was a little boy who lived with his mother and his father in a house with an oven. **(Put the boy, mother, father, and oven in the house and on the board.)**

One day, the mom put a tasty-looking gingerbread man cookie into the oven to bake. **(Put the gingerbread man next to the oven.)**

She said to her own little boy, "You may smell the gingerbread man and you may look at the gingerbread man through the oven window. But you may not take him out of the oven."

The mother went out to work in the garden. The father went out to work in the barn. And the little boy sat down. **(Put the little boy next to the oven. Move the mother and father outside.)**

Pretty soon, a wonderful smell came from the oven. The little boy smelled this wonderful gingerbread smell. He got up to look through the oven window at the gingerbread man. Oh, it looked and smelled so good. The little boy decided to open the oven a teeny tiny bit so that he could get a better smell and a better look. But as soon as he did, do you know what happened?

Yes, the gingerbread man popped right out of the oven and started running across the kitchen floor. "Stop!" yelled the little boy and he started to chase the gingerbread man.

When they ran outside the house, the mother and father ran after the gingerbread man, too. "Stop! Stop!" they yelled. **(Run the mother, father, and boy after the gingerbread man.)**

But the gingerbread man did not stop. Instead he yelled, "Run, run, as fast as you can! You can't catch me. I'm the Gingerbread Man." **(Move the gingerbread man out of the house with the little boy running after him.)**

Soon the gingerbread man came to a cow. When the cow saw him, she said, "Stop, you look delicious! Come on over here." **(Put the cow next to the gingerbread man.)**

But the gingerbread man said, "Oh no! I am not stopping! I have run away from a little boy, and a mother, and a father, and I can run away from you too. So, run, run, as fast as you can! You can't catch me. I'm the Gingerbread Man." **(Move the gingerbread man away from the cow.)**

Soon the gingerbread man came to a pig. When the pig saw him, she said, "Stop, you look delicious! Come on over here." **(Put the pig next to the gingerbread man.)**

But the gingerbread man said, "Oh no! I am not stopping! I have run away from a little boy, and a mother, and a father, and a cow, and I can run away from you too. So, run, run, as fast as you can! You can't catch me. I'm the Gingerbread Man." **(Move the gingerbread man away from the pig.)**

Soon the gingerbread man came to a sheep. When the sheep saw him, she said, "Stop, you look delicious! Come on over here." **(Put the sheep next to the gingerbread man.)**

But the gingerbread man said, "Oh no! I am not stopping! I have run away from a little boy, and a mother, and a father, and a cow, and a pig, and I can run away from you too. So, run, run, as fast as you can! You can't catch me. I'm the Gingerbread Man." **(Move the gingerbread man away from the sheep.)**

Soon the gingerbread man came to a chicken. When the chicken saw him, she said, "Stop, you look delicious! Come on over here." **(Put the chicken next to the gingerbread man.)**

But the gingerbread man said, "Oh no! I am not stopping! I have run away from a little boy, and a mother, and a father, and a cow, and a pig, and a sheep, and I can run away from you too. So, run, run, as fast as you can! You can't catch me. I'm the Gingerbread Man." **(Move the gingerbread man away from the chicken.)**

Finally, the gingerbread man ran past a fox. When the fox saw him, she said, "Stop, you look delicious! Come on over here." **(Put the fox next to the gingerbread man.)**

But the gingerbread man said, "Oh no! I am not stopping! I have run away from a little boy, and a mother, and a father, and a cow, and a pig, and a sheep, and a chicken, and I can run away from you too. So, run, run, as fast as you can! You can't catch me. I'm the gingerbread man." **(Move the gingerbread man away from the fox.)**

The fox said, "What? I can't really hear you. Come a little closer."

So the gingerbread man stopped running. He came a little closer to the fox. In a loud voice, he said, "I have run away from a little boy, and a mother, and a father, and a cow, and a pig, and a sheep, and a chicken, and I can run away from you, too!" **(Move the gingerbread man closer to the fox.)**

But the fox said, "What? I can't really hear you. Come just a little closer, and speak into my ear."

So the gingerbread man came very close to the fox **(Move the gingerbread man closer to the fox.)** and yelled right into the fox's ear, "I have run away from a little boy, and a mother, and a father, and a cow, and a pig, and a sheep, and a chicken, and I can…"

The fox opened his mouth and chomp, chomp. What do you think happened to the gingerbread man?

And that was the end of the gingerbread man.

☸ Discussion Questions ☸

- What happened when the little boy did not obey his mother?

- How did the fox trick the gingerbread man?

Little Red Hen

19

Pictures Needed

- Large House (p. 85–87)
- Hen (p. 51)
- Dog (p. 52)
- Cat (p. 50)
- Pig (p. 59)
- Seeds (p. 72)
- Wheat Plants (p. 72)
- Wheelbarrow (p. 71)
- Oven (p. 67)
- Loaf of Bread (p. 64)

(Put large house and hen on storyboard.)

Once, Little Red Hen lived in a cottage with her friends, Dog, Cat, and Pig. **(Put the dog, cat, and pig in the house.)**

Little Red Hen worked hard around the house. All day long, she cooked, cleaned, and took out the trash. Her friends did not do any of the work.

One day, she found some grains of wheat. **(Put the seeds next to the hen.)** She carried them home and asked her friends, "Who will help me plant these wheat seeds?"

"Not I," said Dog.

"Not I," said Cat.

"Not I," said Pig.

"Very well, then. I will do it myself," she said. And she did.

Soon the wheat seeds started to grow. Little Red Hen said, "Who will help me water the plants and pull the weeds?" **(Put the plants next to the hen.)**

"Not I," said Dog.

"Not I," said Cat.

"Not I," said Pig.

"Very well, then. I will do it myself," she said. And she did.

At the end of the summer, the wheat was very tall and ready to be cut. Little Red Hen said, "Who will help me harvest the wheat?"

"Not I," said Dog.

"Not I," said Cat.

"Not I," said Pig.

"Very well, then. I will do it myself," she said. And she did.

After putting the wheat in a wheelbarrow, Little Red Hen asked, "Who will help me take this wheat to the mill to be ground into flour?" **(Put the wheelbarrow on the board.)**

"Not I," said Dog.

"Not I," said Cat.

"Not I," said Pig.

"Very well, then. I will do it myself," she said. And she did.

When Little Red Hen arrived home from the mill with a big sack of flour, she asked, "Who will help me make this flour into bread?" **(Put the oven on the board.)**

"Not I," said Dog.

"Not I," said Cat.

"Not I," said Pig.

"Very well, then. I will do it myself," she said. And she did.

Soon the kitchen was filled with the wonderful smell of baking bread. At last, the bread was done and ready to be taken from the oven. It was ready to eat! **(Put the loaf of bread on the board.)**

Little Red Hen asked, "Who will help me eat this bread?"

"I will," said Dog.

"I will," said Cat.

"I will," said Pig.

But Little Red Hen said, "All by myself, I planted the seeds. All by myself, I watered and weeded. All by myself, I cut the wheat. All by myself, I took the flour to the mill. All by myself, I baked the bread. And so now, all by myself, I will eat the bread."

And she did.

☺ Discussion Questions ☺

- What should Dog, Cat and Pig have done if they expected to eat the bread?

- Which animal in the cottage was the hardest worker?

- Do you think Dog, Cat and Pig will help next time?

The Magic Fish

20

Pictures Needed

- Hut (p. 82)
- Wife/Mother (p. 45)
- Fisherman in Boat (p. 44)
- Little Fish (p. 52)
- Magic Fish (p. 52)
- Pretty House (p. 82)
- Castle (p. 84)
- Crown (p. 45)
- Cloak (p. 45)

(Put the hut and the wife on the storyboard.)

Far ago there was a fisherman and his wife who lived in a little, old hut by the sea.

(Put fisherman in boat on board.) Every Monday, the wife said to her husband, "Go out to the sea. Go out to the sea and get a fish for me." **(Ask children to repeat this line with you.)** And every Monday, the fisherman came home with a fish. **(Put fish on board.)**

Every Tuesday, she said to her husband, "Go out to the sea. Go out to the sea and get a fish for me." And every Tuesday, the fisherman came home with a fish. **(Put another fish on board.)**

Every Wednesday, she said to her husband, "Go out to the sea. Go out to the sea and get a fish for me." And every Wednesday, the fisherman came home with a fish. **(Put another fish on board.)**

Every Thursday, she said to her husband, "Go out to the sea. Go out to the sea and get a fish for me." And every Thursday, the fisherman came home with a fish. **(Put another fish on board.)**

Every Friday, she said to her husband, "Go out to the sea. Go out to the sea and get a fish for me." But on this Friday, the fisherman came home, but without a fish. His wife was unhappy and demanded to know what happened. The fisherman explained, "I caught a fish today, a big one. It was the biggest one I ever caught. But after I caught him, he told me that he was really a prince in disguise. He asked me to let him go and so I did."

The wife was very angry and said, "Silly man. Why did you let him go? He was a Magic Fish. You should have made a wish. Go back to the fish and tell him that your wife wants a wish. Tell him I wish for a pretty house."

The fisherman said, "I don't want to go."

The wife said, "Go out to the sea. Go out to the sea and get a wish for me." **(Children repeat this new refrain with you.)**

So the fisherman went back to the sea. He called out, "Magic Fish! Magic Fish! My wife wants a wish."

The Magic Fish swam up to the boat. **(Put magic fish on board.)**

"What does your wife want?" asked the Magic Fish.

The fisherman answered, "My wife wants to live in a pretty house, if you please."

"Go home. Your wife's wish has been granted. Now she will live in a pretty house," answered the Magic Fish.

The fisherman rowed home. His wife was waiting there in a pretty house. **(Put the pretty house on the board.)**

The fisherman said, "What a nice house. You will be happy here."

The wife said, "Yes, I will be happy. Probably."

And she was happy—for about a week.

Then she said, "Silly man. Why did you only get one wish from the Magic Fish? Go back to the Magic Fish and tell him that your wife wants another wish. Tell him I wish for a castle."

"I do not want to go," said the fisherman.

The wife said, "Go out to the sea. Go out to the sea and get another wish for me."

So the fisherman went back to the sea. He called out, "Magic Fish! Magic Fish! My wife wants another wish."

The Magic Fish swam up to the boat. **(Put magic fish on board.)**

"What does your wife want?" asked the Magic Fish.

The fisherman answered, "My wife wants to live in a castle, if you please."

"Go home. Your wife's wish has been granted. Now she will live in a castle," answered the Magic Fish.

The fisherman rowed home. His wife was waiting there in the castle. **(Remove the pretty house, and put the castle on the board.)**

The fisherman said, "What a wonderful castle. You will be happy here."

The wife said, "Yes, I will be happy. Probably."

And she was happy—for about two weeks.

Then she said, "Silly man. Why did you only get two wishes from the Magic Fish? Go back to the Magic Fish and tell him that your wife wants another wish. Tell him I wish for to be queen of the land."

"I do not want to go," said the fisherman.

The wife said, "Go out to the sea. Go out to the sea and get a third wish for me."

So the fisherman went back to the sea. He called out, "Magic Fish! Magic Fish! My wife wants a third wish."

The Magic Fish swam up to the boat. **(Put magic fish on board.)**

"What does your wife want?" asked the Magic Fish.

The fisherman answered, "My wife wants to be queen of the land, if you please."

"Go home. Your wife's wish has been granted. Now she will be queen of the land," answered the Magic Fish.

The fisherman rowed home. His wife was there waiting in the castle wearing a beautiful crown and cloak. **(Put a crown and cloak on the wife.)**

The fisherman said, "What a wonderful thing— to be queen of the land. You will be happy."

The wife said, "Yes, I will be happy. Probably."

And she was happy—for about three weeks.

Then she said, "Silly man. Why should I only get three wishes from the Magic Fish? Go back to the Magic Fish and tell him that your wife wants another wish. Tell him I wish to be queen of the sun, and the moon, and the stars."

"I do not want to go," said the fisherman.

The wife said, "Go out to the sea. Go out to the sea and get another wish for me."

So the fisherman went back to the sea. He called out, "Magic Fish! Magic Fish! My wife wants another wish."

The Magic Fish swam up to the boat. **(Put magic fish on board.)**

"What does your wife want?" asked the Magic Fish.

The fisherman answered, "My wife wants to be the queen of the sun, and the moon, and the stars, if you please."

The Magic Fish said, "No. Your wife wants too much. She cannot be queen of the sun, and the moon, and the stars. Now she must go back to the old hut. Go home."

The fisherman rowed home. His unhappy wife was waiting there in the old hut. **(Remove the castle, cloak, and crown, and put the hut on the board.)**

And to this very day, the fisherman and his wife are living in the little old hut by the sea.

 Discussion Questions

- What do you think would make the fisherman's wife happy?

- What would you wish for?

The Monkey and the Tiger

21

Pictures Needed

- Monkey (p. 57–58)
- Tiger (p. 62)
- Bush (p. 73)
- Snake (p. 60)
- Fox (p. 53)
- Cave (p. 79)
- River (p. 77)
- Bear (p. 49)
- Tree (p. 74)
- Lion (p. 55)

One day Little Monkey was playing in the jungle when Tiger crept up behind him. **(Put monkey, tiger and bush on board.)**

"Little Monkey, I am going to eat you up!" roared Tiger.

"Oh, Mr. Tiger, you can't do that to me," whispered Little Monkey.

"Why not eat you? I am hungry," roared Tiger.

Little Monkey had to think of a reason and fast!

Just then, Little Monkey saw a snake slither out from behind a bush. But when the snake saw Tiger, he quietly slithered back into the bush. **(Move snake out and then back into bush.)**

That gave the monkey an idea! Little Monkey said to Tiger, "Mr. Tiger, did you know that I am the most important animal in the jungle? All the other animals are afraid of me."

Tiger did not believe Little Monkey.

Tiger said, "You are too little for any animal to be afraid of you. So, how do I know if you are telling the truth?"

Little Monkey said, "I will show you. I will walk through the jungle and you walk very quietly right behind me. You will see that all the other animals are very afraid of me."

"Very well then," said Tiger. "But it had better be as you say, or you will be my lunch!"

Little Monkey started off through the jungle. Tiger walked right behind him. Soon, they came to a fox sitting outside his cave. **(Put the fox and cave on the board.)**

The fox paid no attention to Little Monkey. But, when he saw Tiger behind Little Monkey, the fox jumped back into his cave very quickly. **(Move fox into cave.)**

Tiger said, "Hmmm…."

Little Monkey walked on. Tiger walked silently right behind him. Soon, they came to a river. **(Put river on the board.)**

A bear was fishing in the river. **(Put bear next to river.)**

Bear gave Little Monkey a glance, but then saw Tiger. Usually, Bear was not afraid of anything! But when he saw Tiger, Bear jumped into the river and swam away! **(Move bear into river.)**

Tiger said, "Hmmm…."

Little Monkey walked on. Tiger walked silently right behind him. Soon, they came to a tree. **(Put tree on board.)**

A lion was sleeping under the tree. **(Put lion under tree.)**

Lion opened one eye and saw Little Monkey. Then Lion opened the other eye and saw Tiger.

Lion roared at him. **(Move lion away from Tiger.)**

Tiger was very impressed. "Hmmm…I see that even Lion is afraid of you, Little Monkey. Perhaps you are important. Perhaps, I should not eat you, at least, not today. You may go, Little Monkey. But watch out for me; I may decide to eat you tomorrow!"

☼ Discussion Questions ☼

- How did Little Monkey's trick work on Tiger?
- Were the fox, bear and lion really afraid of Little Monkey?

Too Noisy

Pictures Needed

- Large House (p. 85–87)
- Farmer/Father (p. 45)
- Wife/Mother (p. 45)
- Girl (p. 42)
- Plates (p. 68)
- Dog (p. 52)
- Cow (p. 51)
- Chicken (p. 51)
- Pig (p. 59)
- Sheep (p. 60)

(Place the large house and the farmer on the storyboard.)

Far ago, there was a little house. A farmer lived in the little house with his wife and their daughter.

All day long, the girl played and sang, and the wife clattered her dishes as she cooked and cleaned. The farmer thought that it was too noisy! He wanted it to be quiet! **(Place the wife, girl, and plates on the board.)**

The farmer went to the wise man. He said, "My house is too noisy! All day long my little girl plays and sings. All day long my wife clatters the dishes. I need quiet!"

The wise man asked, "Do you have a dog?"

"Yes, but how will a dog help?" answered the farmer.

The wise man replied, "Bring your dog into your house."

The farmer said, "My dog is an outside dog and he is very big. And his bark is even bigger! How will that help?"

"It will help," replied the wise man.

(Put the dog in the house.)

All day long the next day, the girl played and sang, the wife clattered her dishes, and the dog barked.

The farmer went back to the wise man. He said, "My house is too noisy! All day long my little girl plays and sings. All day long my wife clatters the dishes. All day long the dog barks. I need quiet!"

The wise man asked, "Do you have a cow?"

"Yes, you know I do! It moos all day long. But how will a cow help?" asked the farmer.

"It will help. Bring your cow into the house," replied the wise man.

(Put the cow in the house.)

All day long the next day, the girl played and sang, the wife clattered her dishes, the dog barked, and the cow mooed.

The farmer went back to the wise man. He said, "My house is too noisy! All day long my little girl plays and sings. All day long my wife clatters the dishes. All day long the dog barks. All day long the cow moos. I need quiet!"

The wise man asked, "Do you have a chicken?"

"Yes, my chicken clucks every time she lays an egg. But how will a chicken help?"

"It will help. Bring your chicken into your house," ordered the wise man. **(Put the chicken in the house.)**

All day long the next day, the girl played and sang, the wife clattered her dishes, the dog barked, the cow mooed, and the chicken clucked.

The farmer went back to the wise man. He said, "My house is too noisy! All day long my little girl plays and sings. All day long my wife clatters the dishes. All day long the dog barks. All day long the cow moos. All day long the chicken clucks. I need quiet!"

The wise man asked, "Do you have a pig?"

"Yes, he is the loudest oinker in the world. But how will a pig help?"

"It will help. Bring your pig into your house," ordered the wise man. **(Put the pig in the house.)**

All day long the next day, the girl played and sang, the wife clattered her dishes, the dog barked, the cow mooed, the chicken clucked, and the pig oinked.

The farmer went back to the wise man. He said, "My house is too noisy! All day long my little girl plays and sings. All day long my wife clatters the dishes. All day long the dog barks. All day long the cow moos. All day long the chicken clucks. All day long the pig oinks. I need quiet!"

The wise man asked, "Do you have sheep?"

"Yes, but my sheep drive me crazy with their baa, baaing. How will sheep help?"

"They will help. Bring your sheep into your house," ordered the wise man. **(Put the sheep in the house.)**

All day long the next day, the girl played and sang, the wife clattered her dishes, the dog barked, the cow mooed, the chicken clucked, the pig oinked, and the sheep baa, baaed.

The farmer went back to the wise man. He said, "My house is too noisy! All day long my little girl plays and sings. All day long my

wife clatters the dishes. All day long the dog barks. All day long the cow moos. All day long the chicken clucks. All day long the pig oinks. All day long the sheep baa, baa. I came to you because I wanted quiet! But my house is noisier than ever. I need quiet!"

The wise man answered, "Here is what you should do. Put the sheep out. Put the cow out. Put the pig out. Put the chicken out. Put the dog out."

"Very well," answered the farmer. He went home and he put the sheep, cow, pig, chicken, and dog out of his house.

(One by one, take these animals off the board.)

All day long, the girl played and sang, and the wife clattered her dishes. The farmer thought that it was soooo quiet.

And that's the story of "Too Noisy!"

☼ Discussion Questions ☼

- Was the house really more quiet than it was at the beginning of the story?

- Why did the farmer think it was quieter?

- Why did the wise man want the farmer to bring the animals into the house? How did this help?

Story Patterns

These patterns are organized into two main sections: "Characters" and "Props and Scenery." You may enlarge or shrink the items to fit your individual needs.

Characters

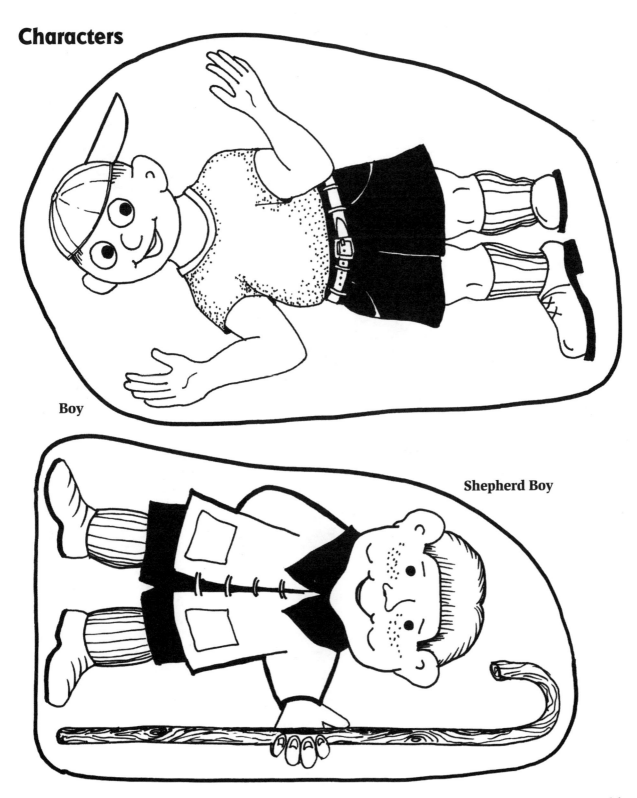

Boy

Shepherd Boy

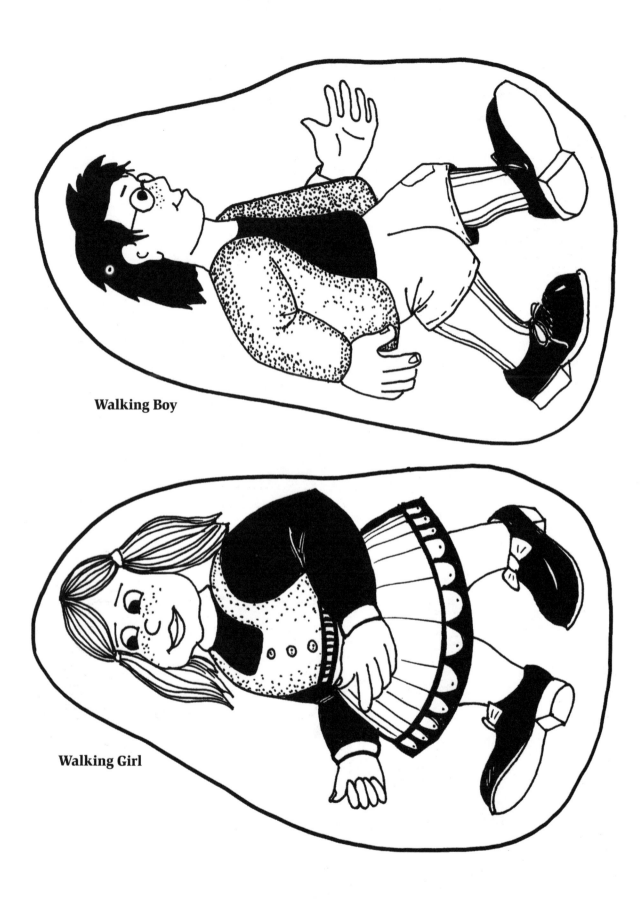

Walking Boy

Walking Girl

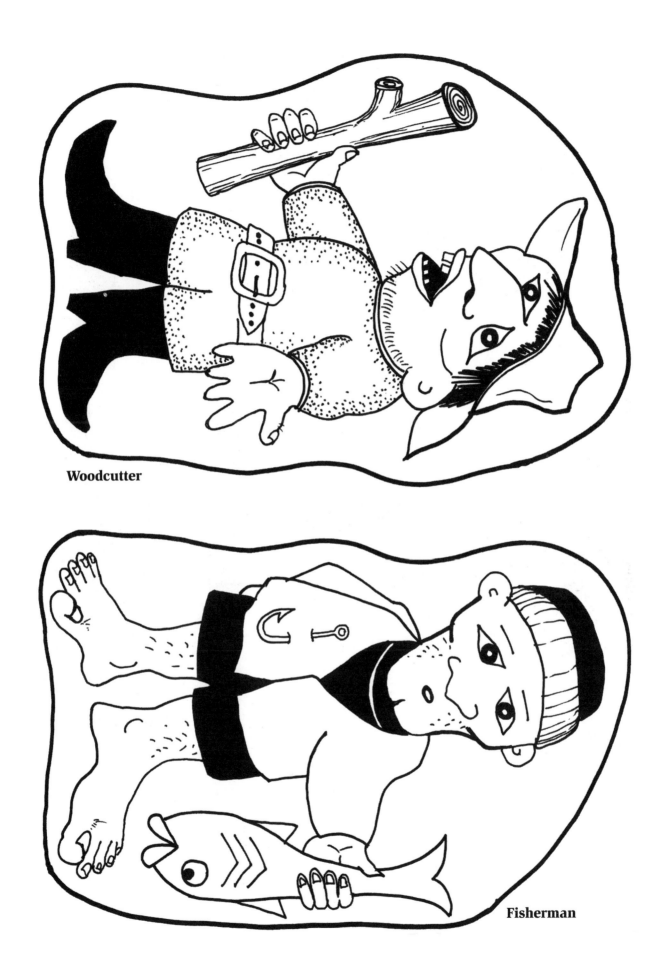

Woodcutter

Fisherman

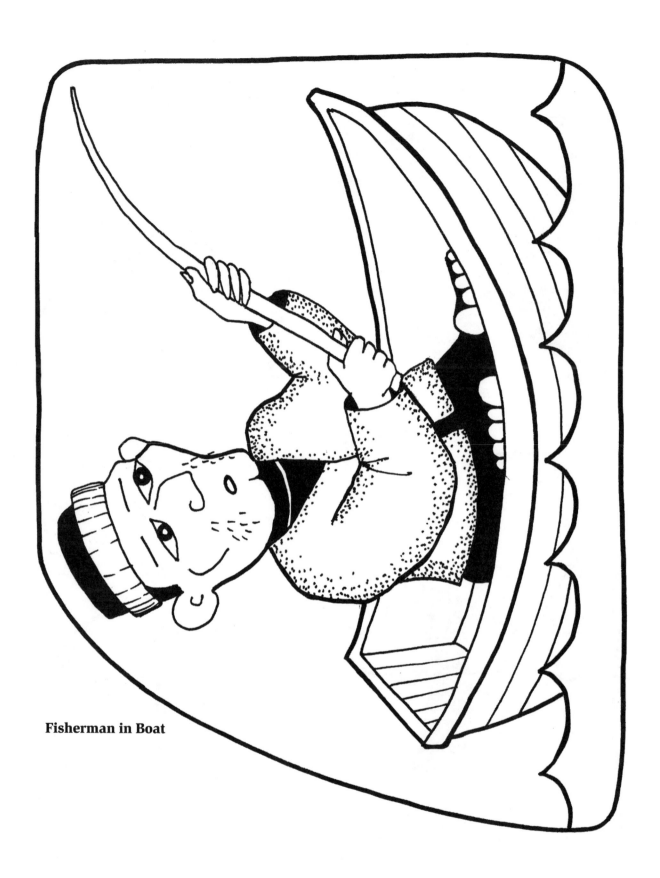

Fisherman in Boat

Farmer/Father

Wife/Mother

Cloak for Wife

Crown for Wife

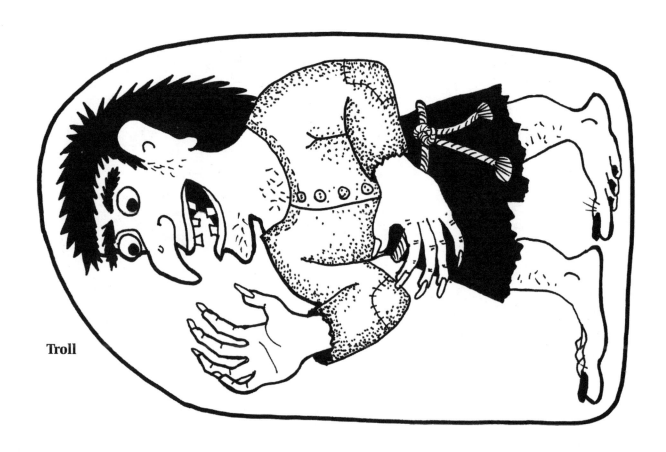

Troll

Leprechaun

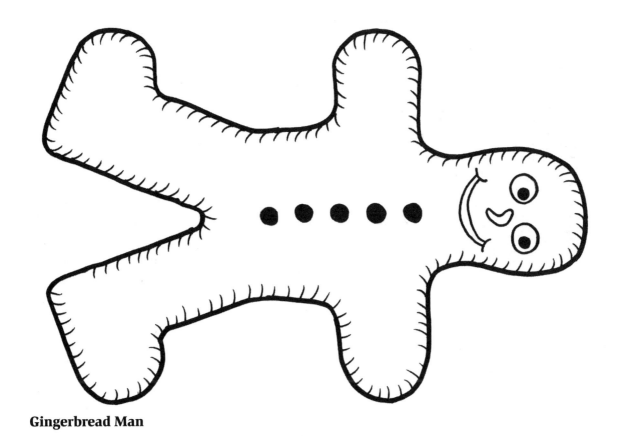

Gingerbread Man

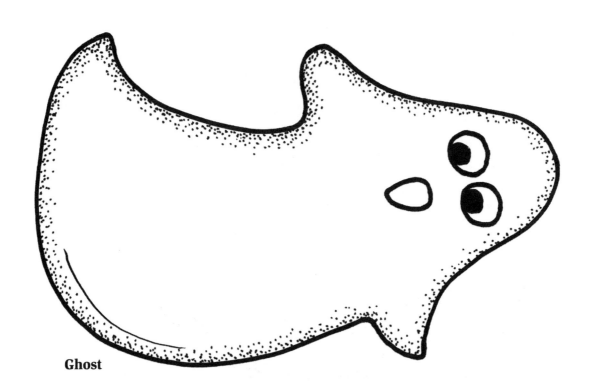

Ghost

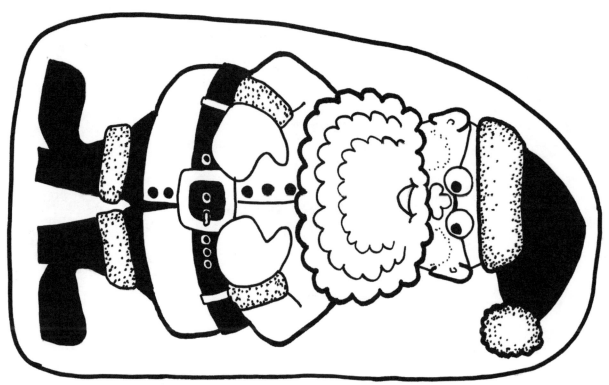

Santa

Snowman

Bear

Teddy Bear

Bunny/Hare

Cat

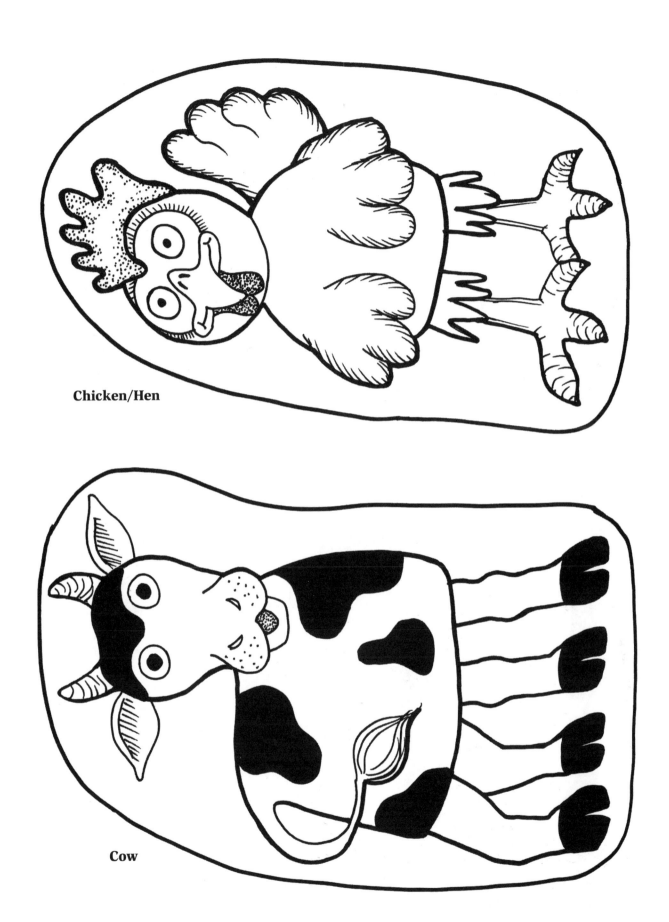

Chicken/Hen

Cow

Dog

Magic Fish

Little Fish

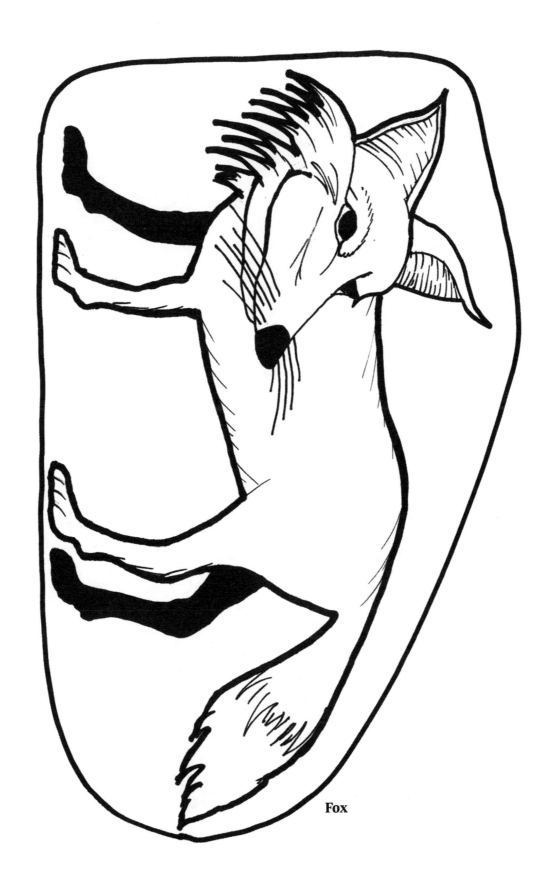

Fox

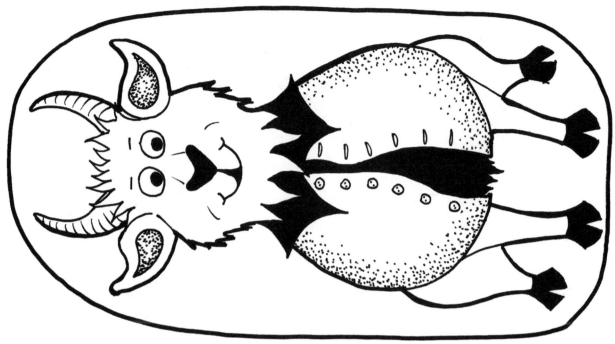

Large Goat

Middle Goat

Small Goat

Lion

Mouse

Mice

Monkeys

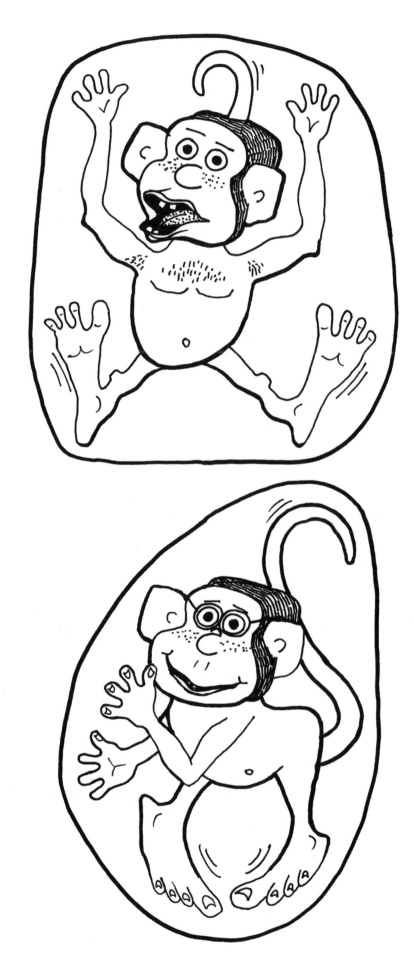

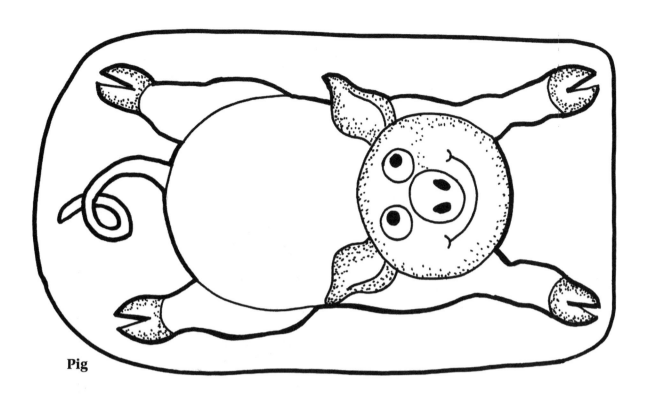

Pig

Reindeer

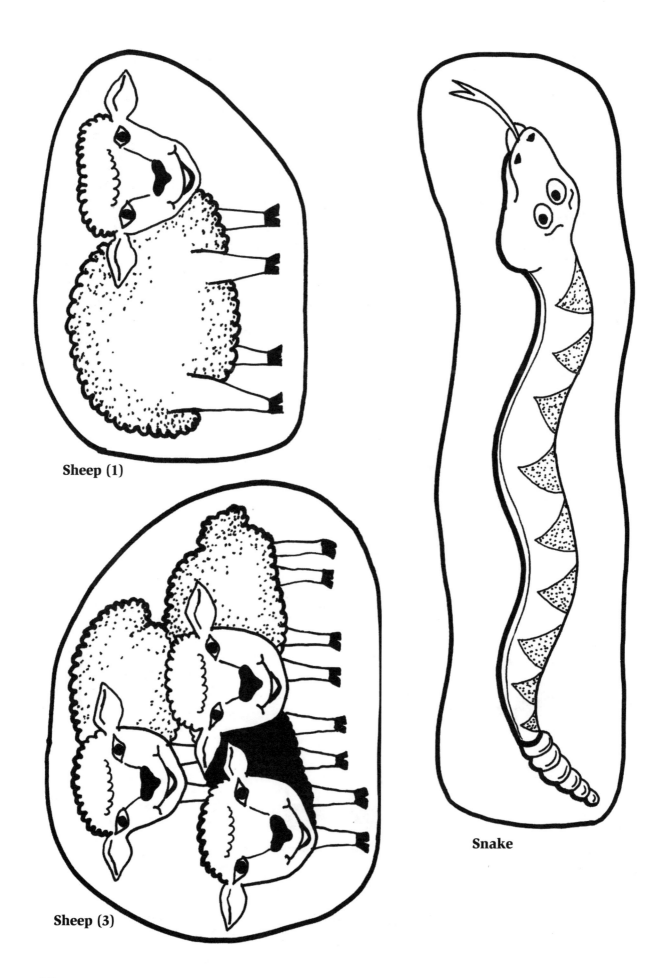

Sheep (1)

Sheep (3)

Snake

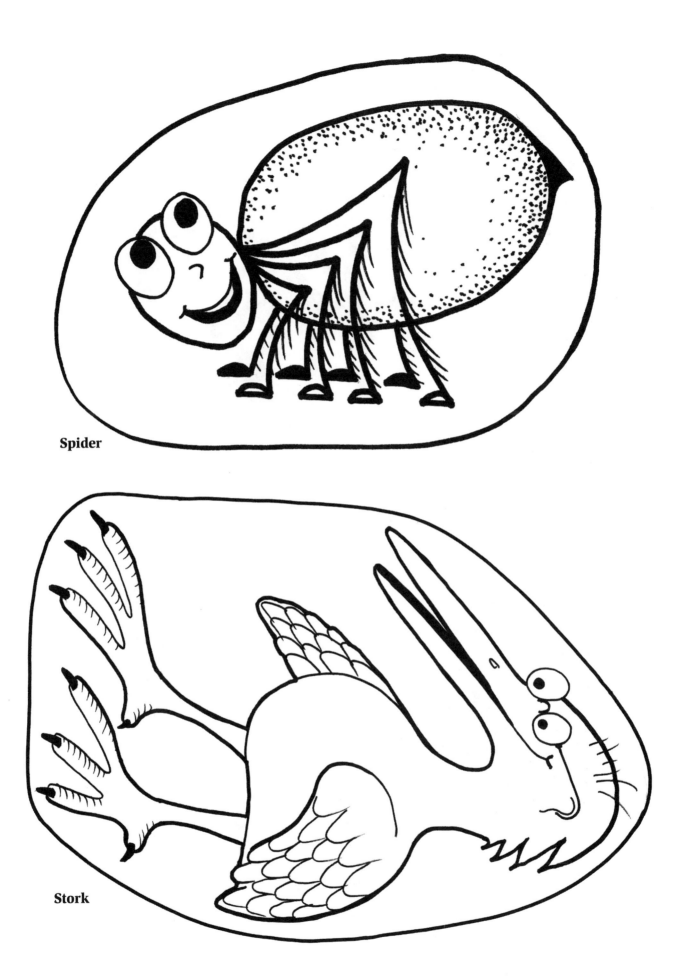

Spider

Stork

Tiger

Turkey

Tortoise/Turtle

Wolf

Props and Scenery

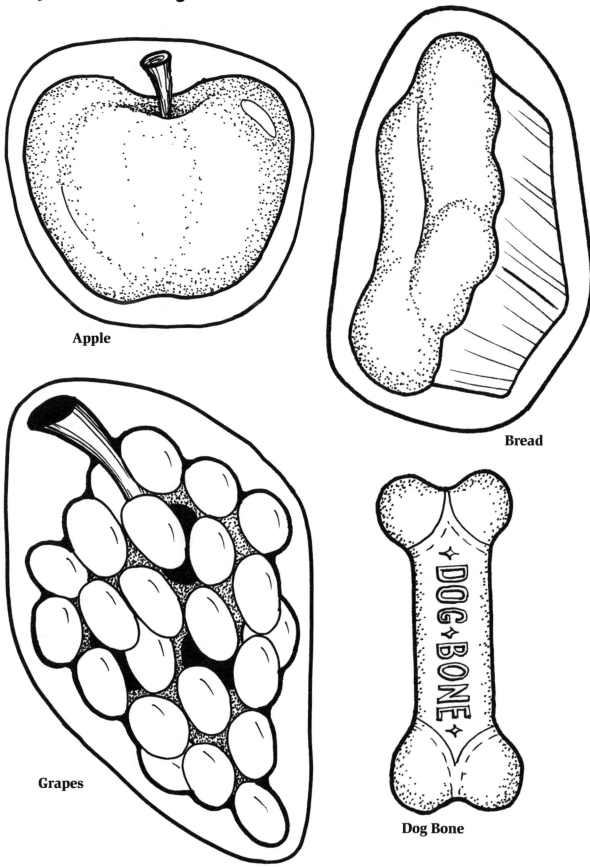

Apple

Bread

Grapes

Dog Bone

Pumpkin

Jack-O-Lantern

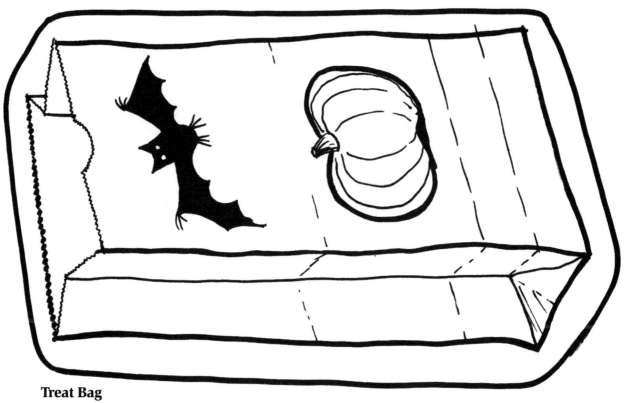

Treat Bag

Candy

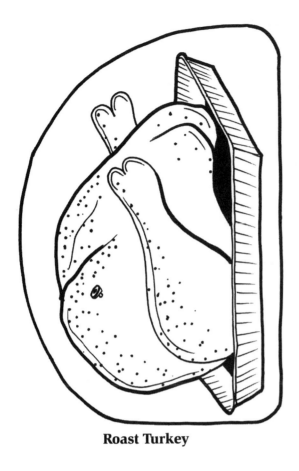

Roast Turkey

Oven

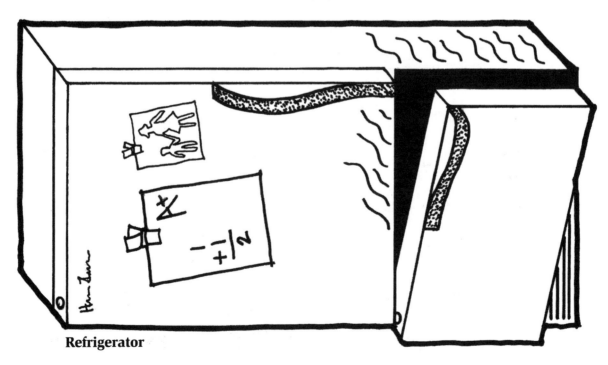

Refrigerator

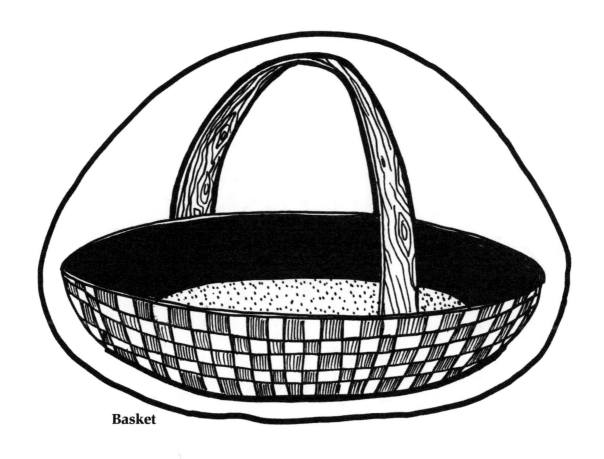

Basket

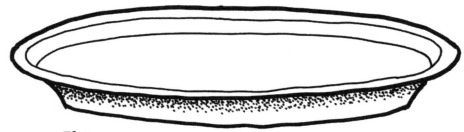

Plate

Tall Glass

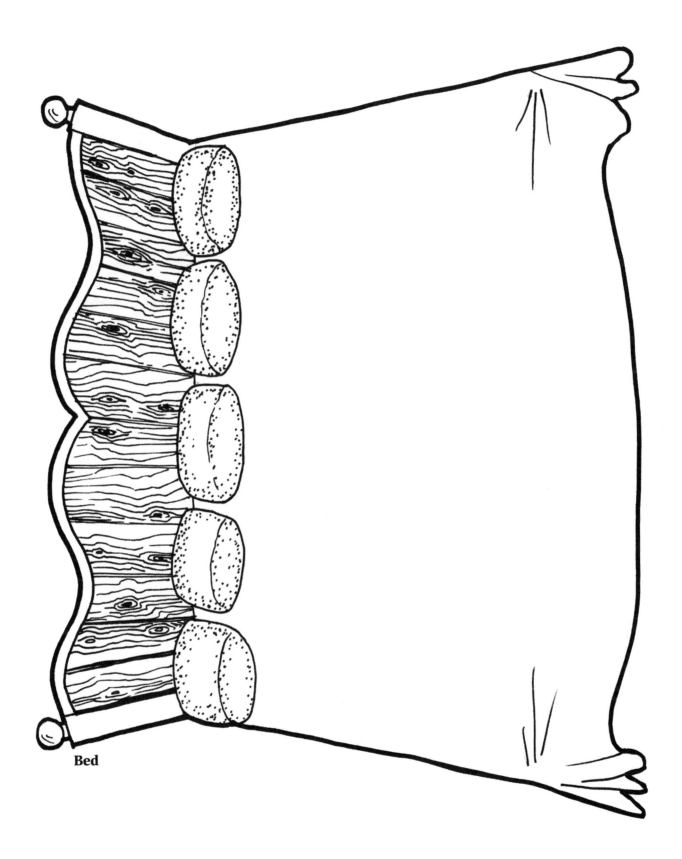

Bed

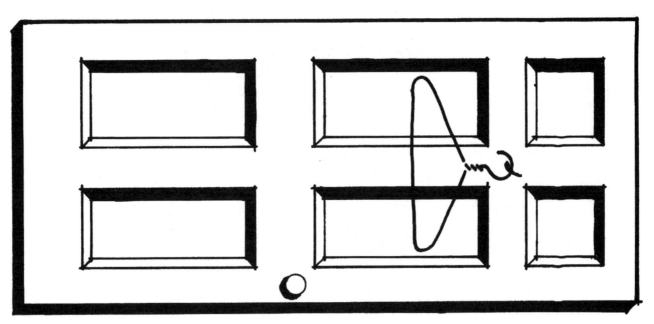

Closet Door

Present

Valentine

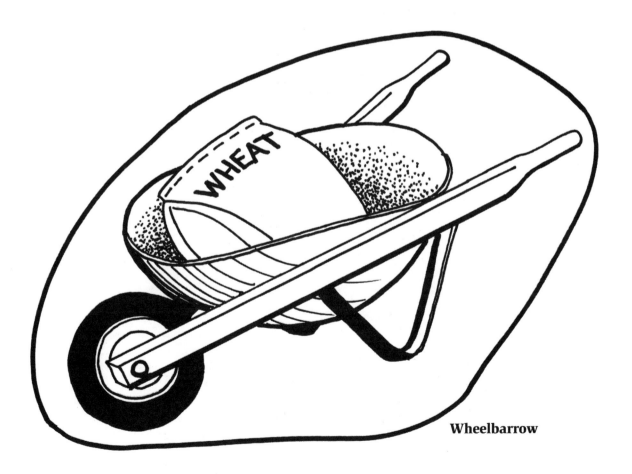

Wheelbarrow

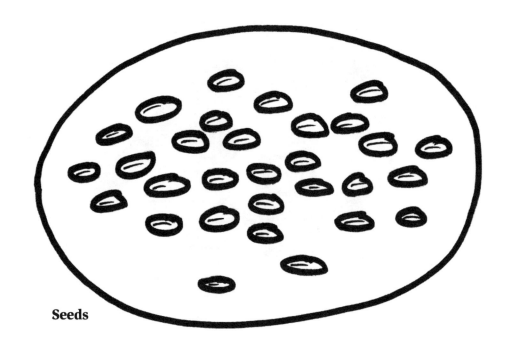

Seeds

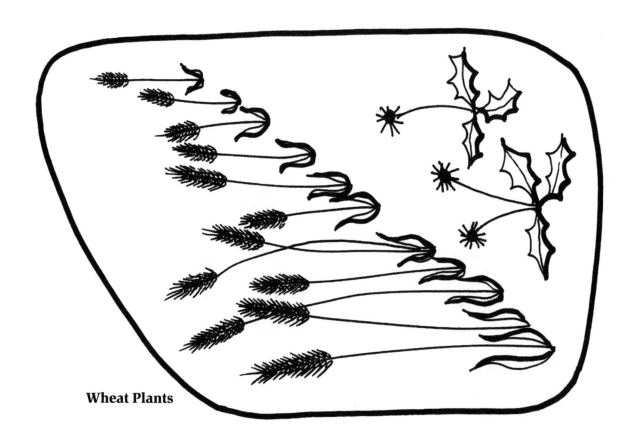

Wheat Plants

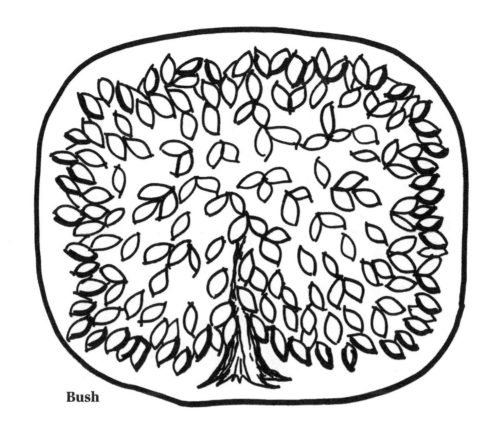

Bush

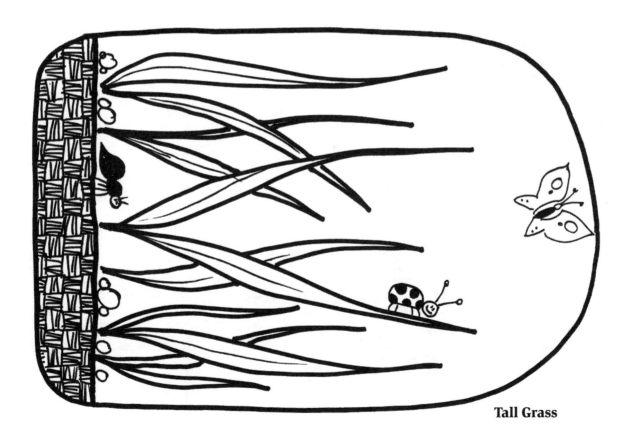

Tall Grass

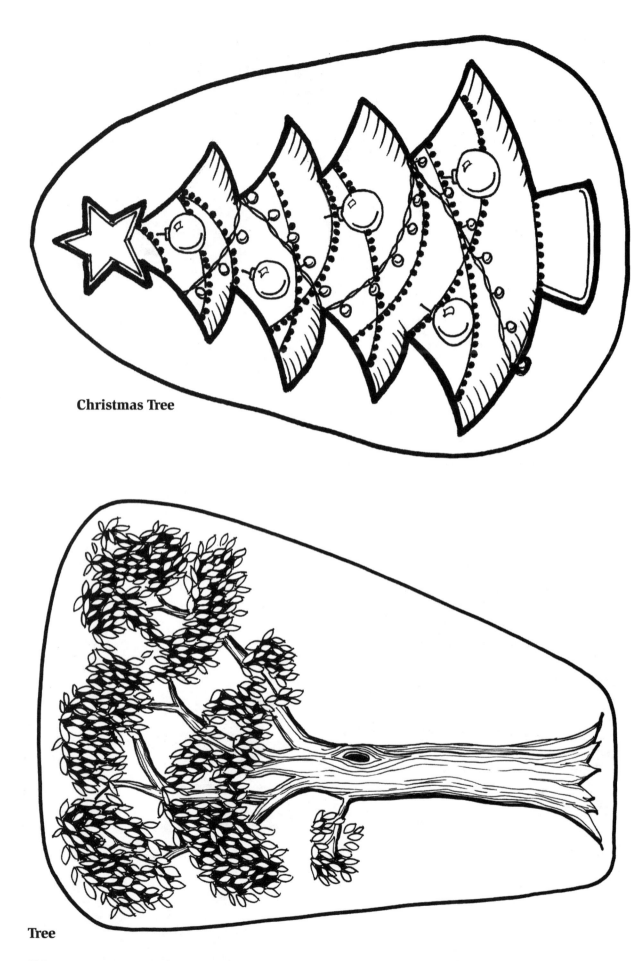

Christmas Tree

Tree

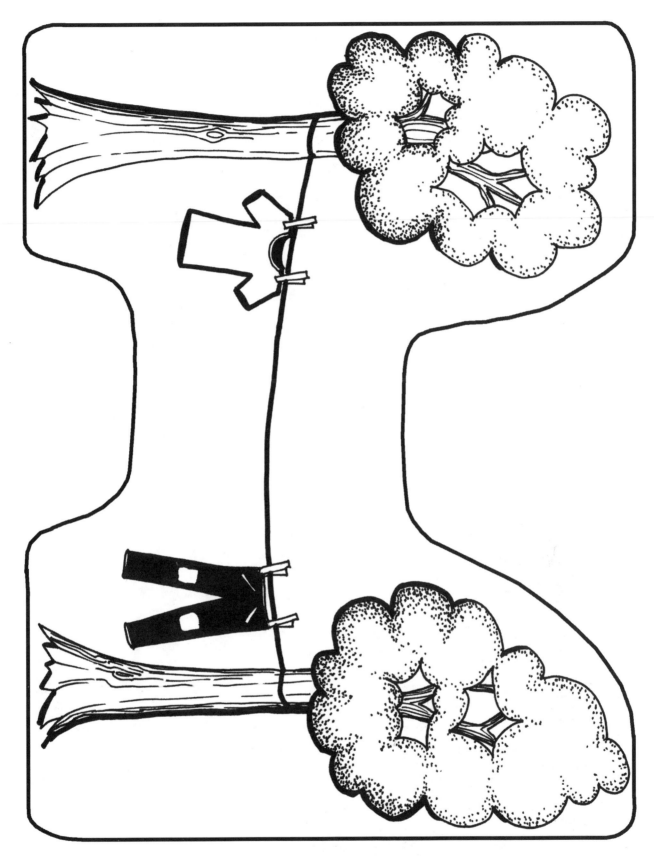

Clothesline

Rain Cloud

Sun

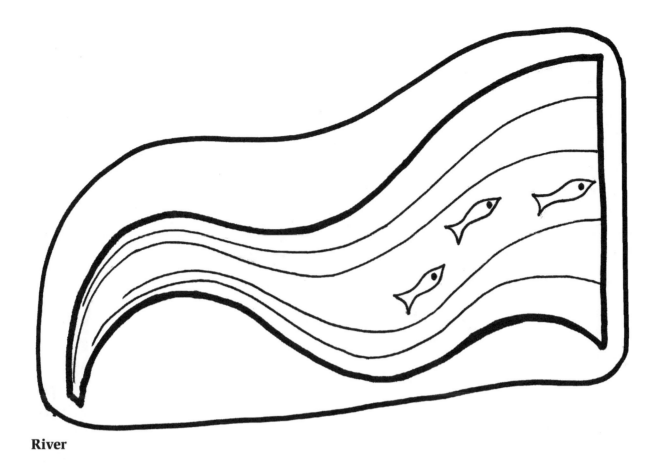

River

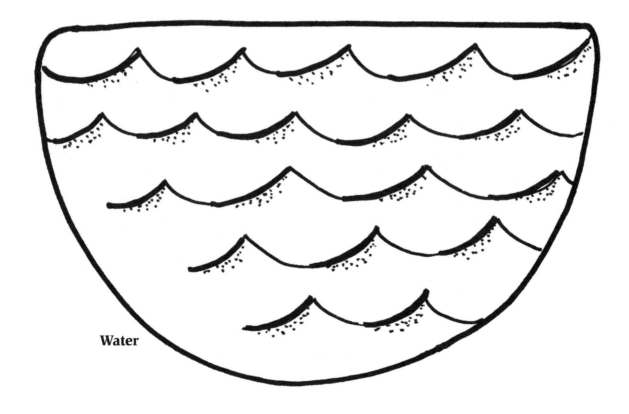

Water

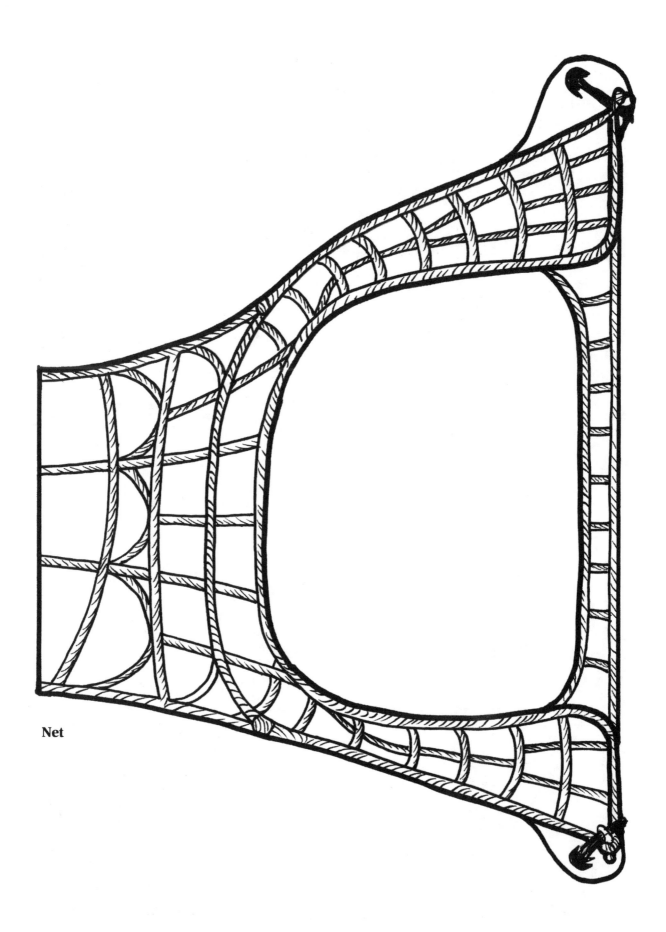

Net

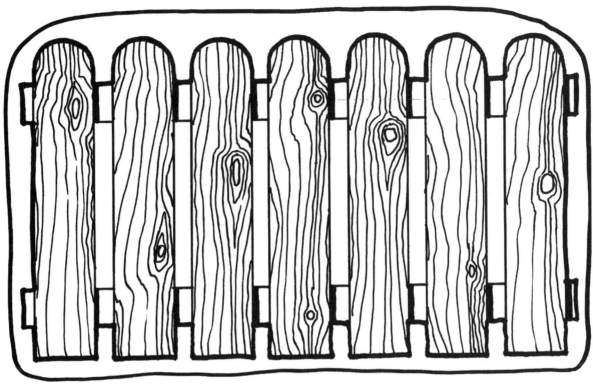

Fence

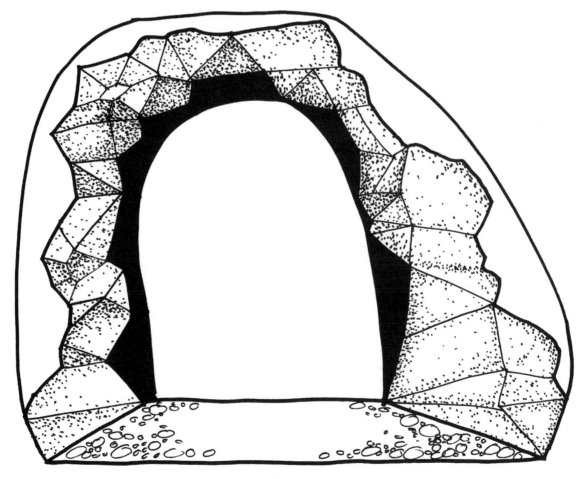

Cave

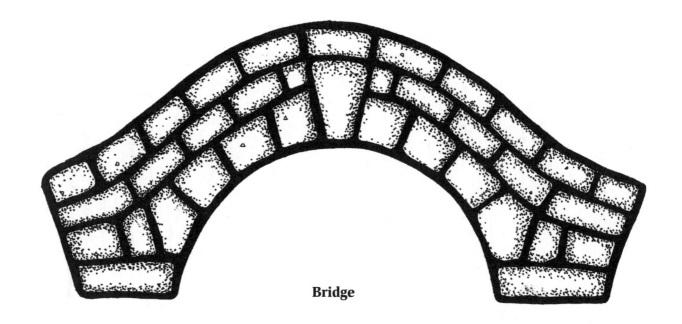

Bridge

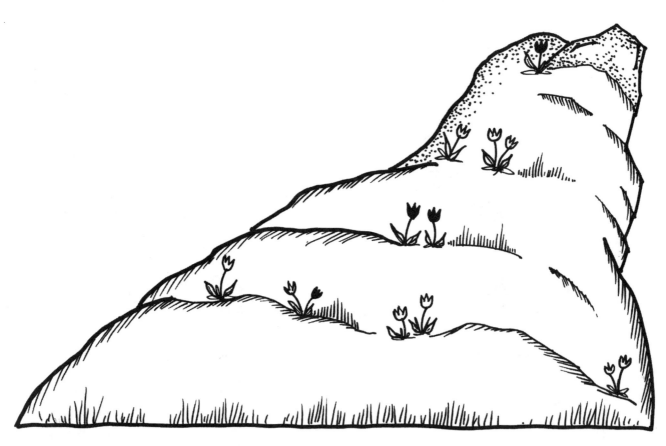

Mountain/Hill

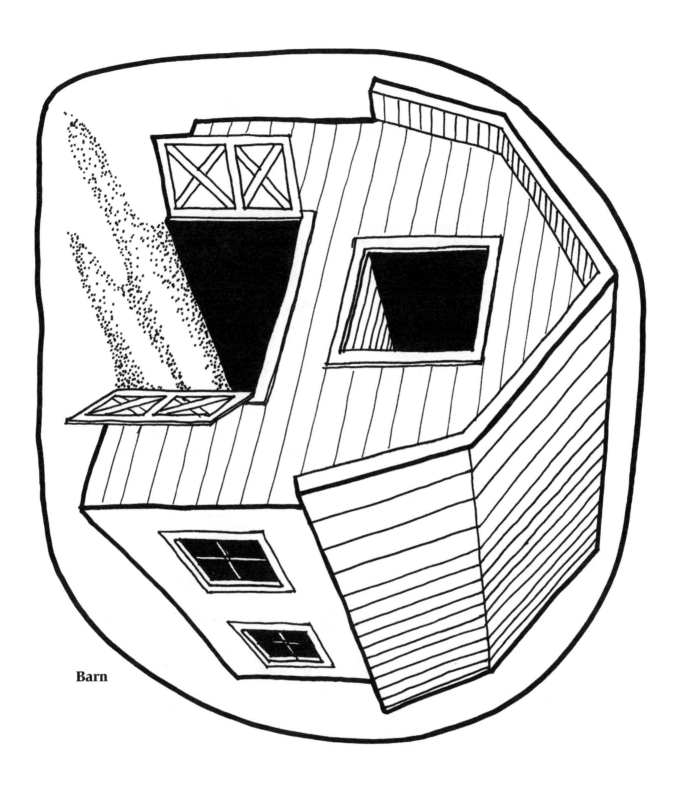

Barn

Hut

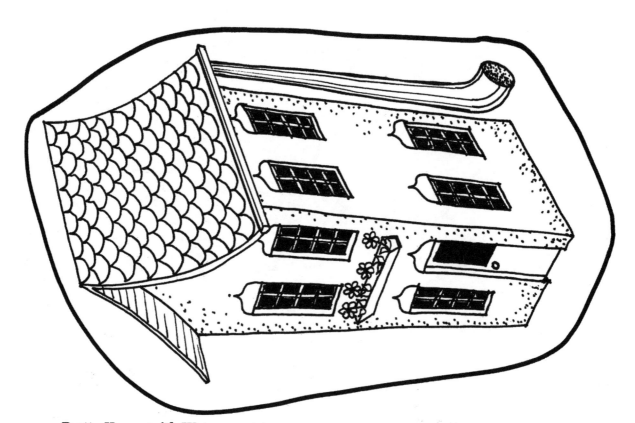

Pretty House with Waterspout

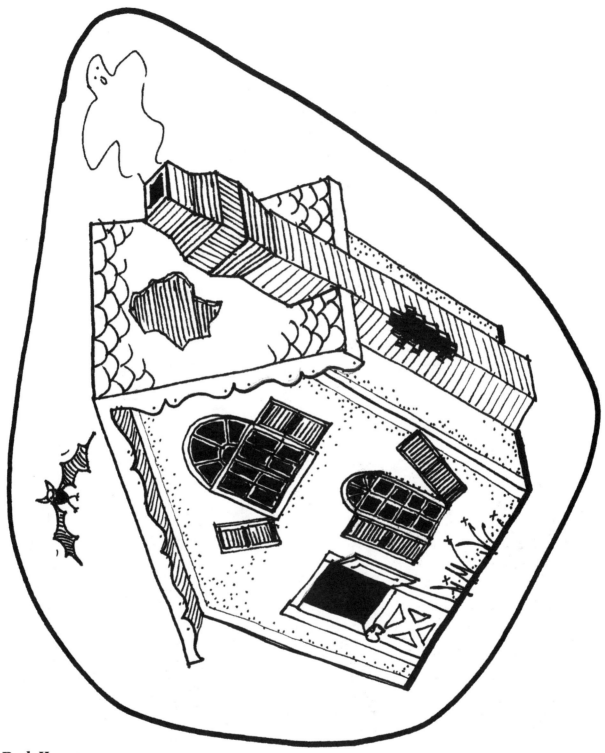

Dark House

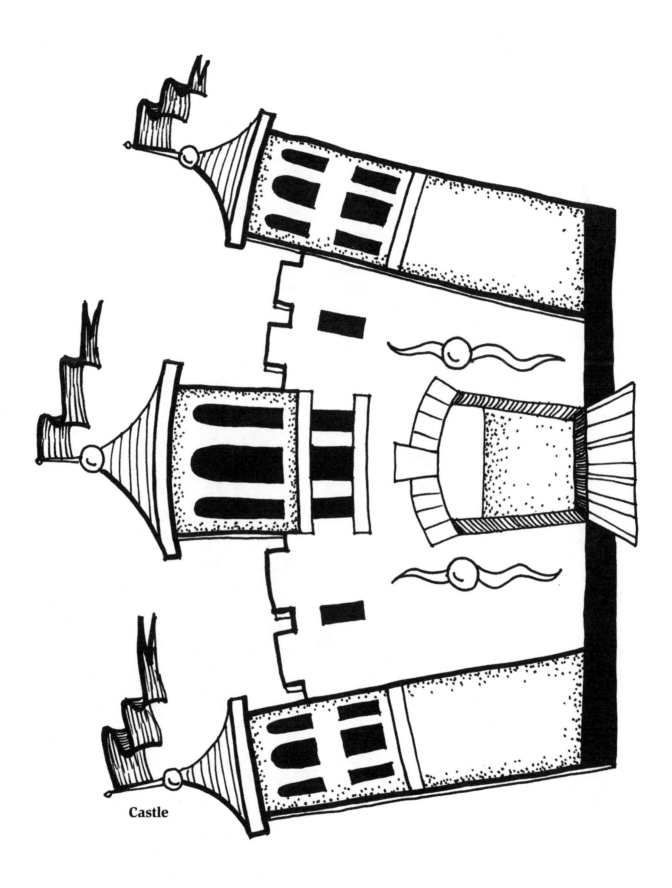

Castle

Large House A

Large House B

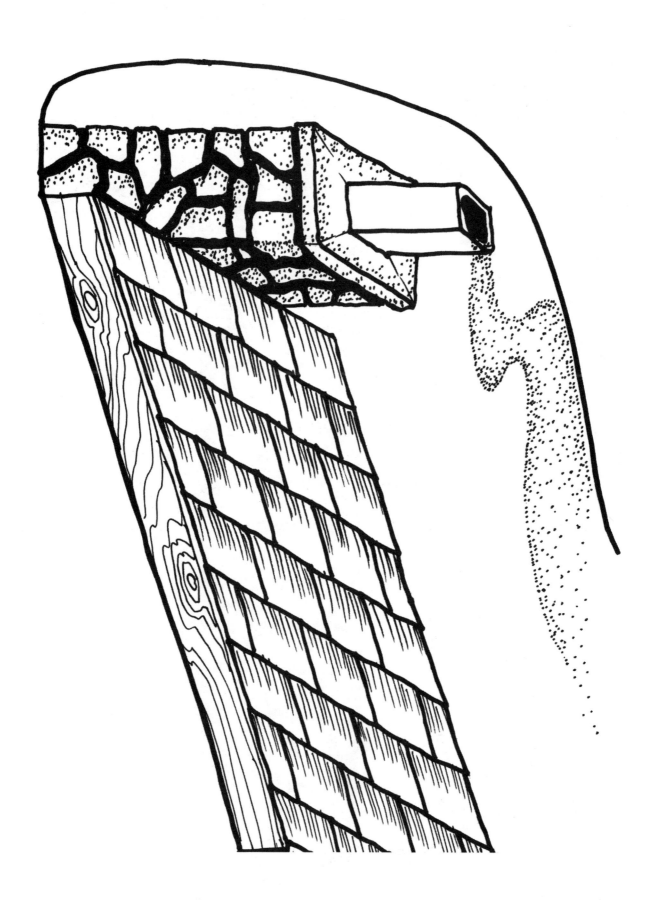

Large House C

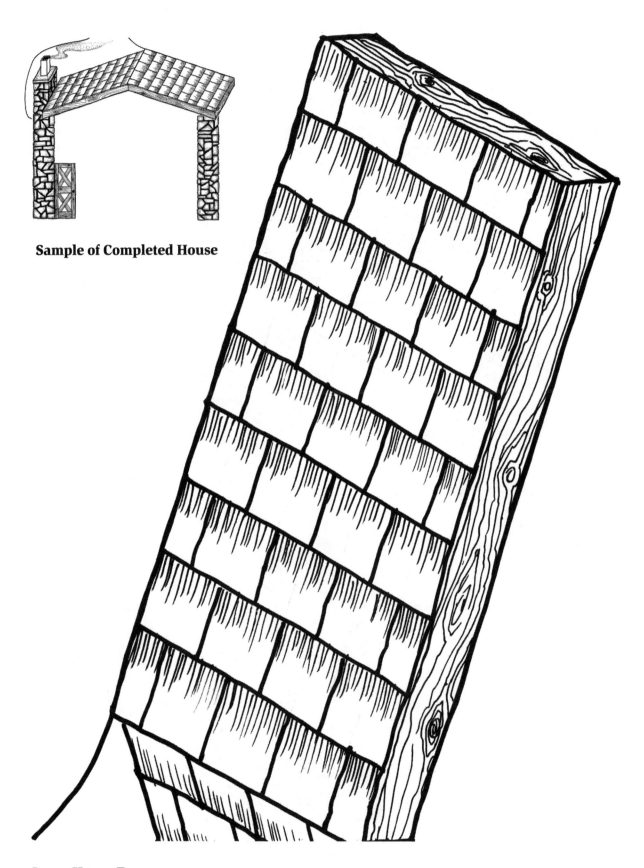

Sample of Completed House

Large House D

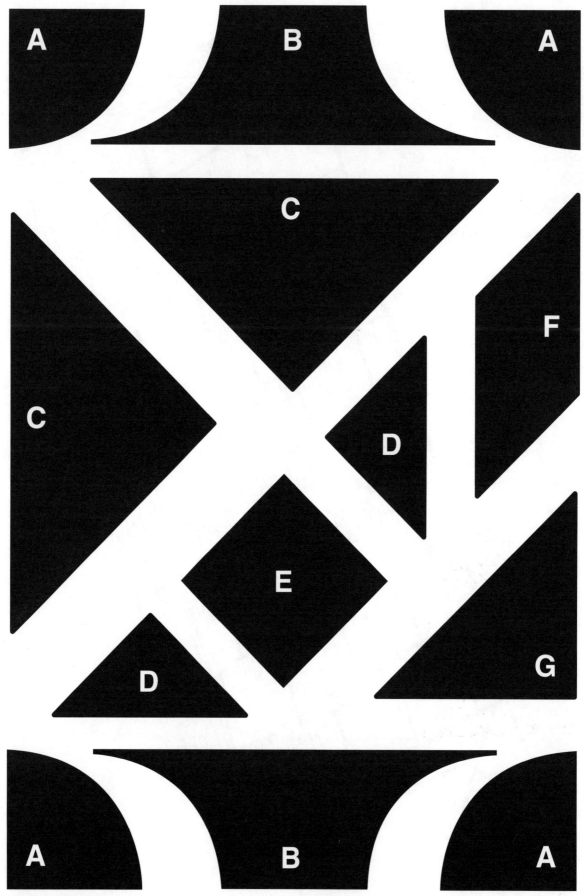

Tangram Pieces